# Go from Space Age to Stone Age —and Survive!

**With a few simple raw materials—primarily wood, stone, bone, animal tissues, and plant fibers—you can be self-sufficient in the primitive wilderness.**

At Brigham Young University, Larry Olsen established the award-winning course called "Youth Rehabilitation Through Outdoor Survival." After taking the course, one of Olsen's thousands of students wrote: "We hadn't food, bedding, or implements of any kind—just the shirts on our backs —and we survived! We learned a deep respect for human life and nature."

# LARRY DEAN OLSEN

# OUTDOOR SURVIVAL SKILLS

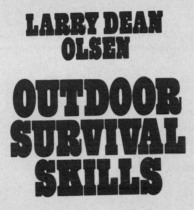

PUBLISHED BY POCKET BOOKS NEW YORK

POCKET BOOKS, a division of Simon & Schuster, Inc.
1230 Avenue of the Americas, New York, N.Y. 10020

Fourth edition © 1973 by Brigham Young University Press;
previous editions copyright © 1967, 1969, 1970 by Brigham Young
University Press

Published by arrangement with Brigham Young University Press
Library of Congress Catalog Card Number: 72-94938

ISBN: 0-671-54316-4

First Pocket Books printing June, 1976

17   16   15   14   13   12   11   10   9

Front cover photograph: Four by Five

POCKET and colophon are registered trademarks
of Simon & Schuster, Inc.

Printed in the U.S.A.

## PICTURE CREDITS

Pictures by Dan Smith, Jr., Nature Graphics, Provo, Utah, except for
Figs. 1-4, 23, and 47: Stan Macbean
Figs. 22, 26, 114, and 152: Pat Wright
Figs. 35, 93, and 94: Larry Dean Olsen
Fig. 42: Robert Paul Milberg
Figs. 59 and 76: Doug Martin, Martin Photographics, Provo, Utah
All drawings in the Appendix: Lauren Jarrett

To my father

NIMIIMPU · HI·TO · TEACH · TO SURVIVE · LEARN · TO

# CONTENTS

# FOREWORD

A sad notion prevails in many circles today that the answer to our future is in our past. Certainly we have made a mess of things in terms of the environment we are to live in. Just where we are going in this direction is a question we should all ask ourselves. Where, after all, has modern technology led us regarding the air we breathe, the food we eat, and the land we live on?

This question is of major importance in *Jeremiah Johnson,* a film that director Sydney Pollack and I made for Warner Bros. The disregard for the environment today is pronounced by the high regard the early trappers had for the land yesterday. In order to properly document a single man's struggles for survival in the wilderness we wanted to have a technical adviser—someone who could give us detailed facts about how a man really did build a fire, set a trap, build shelter, shore up against the elements.

Since my home is in the mountains in Utah, I have become acquainted with the survival programs of Larry Dean Olsen at Brigham Young University in Provo and

I believe his book *Outdoor Survival Skills* to be the finest of its kind. I contacted Mr. Olsen and asked if he would serve as our technical consultant. He gladly obliged and his efforts have given us a truthful and interesting documentation of an early life-style in America. His knowledge of man's conditioning to snow and the high country as well as to heat and the barren desert country is enormous. As an actor, I am very concerned about detail and authenticity, and I am comfortable that the accounts of an early life-style in this film are accurate. Mr. Olsen's tireless efforts and superior ability have made this possible.

Robert Redford
Warner Bros. Studios
Burbank, California

*Editorial Comment: In an age characterized by leisure, most people depend too much on push buttons, time clocks, and other indoor conveniences for their daily survival. Consequently, they do not develop the abilities or skills which could enable them to survive stresses encountered in the wilds. History is full of war-ruined civilizations that have fallen from indoor luxury to outdoor desperation in only a few hours.*

*For the Stone Age man, necessity was the mother of invention, and he adapted to her toughest demands. Today, however, the mother of invention is probably leisure—or it can be if man deliberately uses that leisure to seek challenge. If he desires to combine the toughness of his ancestors with his own intellectual prowess in order to become a fully developed man prepared for the worst or the best, he is wise; he learns from yesterday.* Outdoor Survival Skills *allows today's reader to bridge the gap.*

*The author, Larry Dean Olsen, born and raised in Idaho, became interested early in his desert environment and the material culture of the ancient Indian inhabitants of the West. This led him to an intensive study of their lifeways—he tested all aspects of their survival skills by trekking into the remote canyon areas of the western deserts and experiencing survival at its most primitive level. Using tools and weapons of stone and bone, digging roots and trapping game with primitive implements and traps, suffering cold nights without bedding and hot days without water or even shoes, Larry has gained a unique concept of man in nature.*

*In 1966 Larry began teaching classes in outdoor survival in the Division of Continuing Education at Brigham Young University in Provo, Utah, sponsored by the Department of Youth Leadership. His caveman approach to survival, based on the idea that survival training is best achieved by learning to live off the land without previously manufactured gear, has won wide approval. His lectures and wilderness laboratories, which focus primarily on survival in the western United States, have been highly valuable to participants. Even the few who have found it difficult to "eat to live" rather than to "live to eat" have gained a respect for nature and the way that man can be a part of it. Larry's mastery of primitive skills has made him confident that survival living need not be an ordeal once a person has learned to adjust to the plunge from the present into the past.*

*In 1967 Larry established a course in the Department of Youth Leadership at BYU under the title "Youth*

*Rehabilitation through Outdoor Survival." More than
2,000 students have participated in his wilderness laboratories, field-testing his concepts. Enthusiastic about
the results, many upon returning have commented with
awe: "We hadn't food, shoes, bedding, or implements
of any kind. Just the shirts on our backs—and we survived!" This national award-winning course uses the
stress of actual 26-day trips into the mountains and
deserts of the West as a living experience for both
leaders and youth. The program has opened up a new
area in survival training by providing a vehicle for
leaders to help young men and women establish lasting
values, exercise courage in the face of seemingly insur-
mountable obstacles, and, above all, develop a com-
passionate respect for human life and its relationship
to nature.*

*The book itself has created an enthusiasm for outdoor
education concepts. Each year the Department of Youth
Leadership at BYU receives numerous requests for this
national best-seller which has become a favorite of Boy
Scouts all over America. Outdoor Survival Skills is also
well known to the National Parks Service and is sold in
England and Canada. The new edition has been de-
signed with new print and new art to help the reader
find more quickly the information he will need in a
wide variety of outdoor survival situations. It is written
primarily for the young men and young women who will
readily adapt it to their needs.*

# ACKNOWLEDGMENTS

The very nature of presenting a publication based on personal experiences and training must involve the participants who shared those moments. My wife, Sherrel, has cooked my meals for many moons in caves and under open skies. Lonny Paul Newman has accompanied me on some of the most severe tests of living off the land. Jim L. Winder, a skilled hunter and endurer, has tested with me some of the materials discussed herein. Robert L. Burnham has been my companion in primitive living and has shared his skills with me. Norman Herrett of the Herrett Arts and Science Center in Twin Falls, Idaho, has brought to the public a form of education that makes the primitive mind live in the minds of people today. Richard A. Olsen has been an early example and teacher in the ways of a hunter and trapper. Thomas A. James and Thane J. Packer first encouraged me in the idea that outdoor survival should be offered in the education of all people, and helped to see it made possible on the Brigham Young University campus. Fred Bohman has given me valuable technical assistance on plants and pictures. Dan Smith of Nature Graphics, Provo, Utah, is responsible for most of the pictures. William Whitaker has supplied the sketches. To all of these people and to the more than 2,000 students who have field-tested the concepts in this book—thanks.

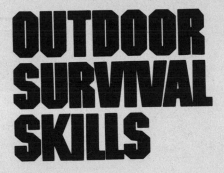

# OUTDOOR SURVIVAL SKILLS

**1**

Fig. 1. The author straightening an arrow shaft

# INTRODUCTION

## Philosophy of a Caveman

Survival studies have shown that those who adapt successfully in a stress situation share some common attributes which set them apart from those who don't. A survivor possesses determination, a positive degree of stubbornness, well-defined values, self-direction, and a belief in the goodness of mankind. He is also cooperative. He does not feel that man's basic nature is to promote only self-interest; instead, he believes that most men are good and concerned about other people. Consequently, he is active in daily life and is usually a leader, though he may also belong to groups as a strong follower.

A survivor is also kind to himself. He does not fear pain or discomfort, nor does he seek to punish himself with them. He is not a self-hater. Even the most difficult existence is acceptable to him if it is beyond his ability to change it. Otherwise he will fight for change. He knows the odds.

Because an aura of timelessness exists in a survival situation, a person cannot allow himself to be over-

**Fig. 3. Using a flint knife**

**Fig. 2. Sharpening a stone knife**

**Fig. 4. Starting a fire with the bow drill**

come by the duration or the quality of his existence. A survivalist accepts it as it is and improves it from that standpoint. One of civilized man's greatest weaknesses in a stress condition is his lack of ability to do this easily. If punching a time clock improves efficiency, it may conversely jangle a man's ability to endure to the end —that is, if he lets it.

A survivor also possesses a utopian attitude. This is not a reflection of any comfort orientation but is evidence of an artistic nature. He makes even the most miserable existence seem like millennial splendor. I have witnessed this in my best students. Their digging sticks are works of art, their deadfalls ingenious, and their camps miracles of compactness and industry. There is nothing crude in the primitive existence of these people.

Stone Age living implies two things: first, an immersion within the affective domain of life and secondly,

Fig. 5. Using an automatic pump drill

a life centered away from comfort and ease. Reasons for this may rest in meaning and time.

Affective living places some of the meanings of life in the world of work—of doing. Priorities in a hand-to-mouth existence quickly force industry to an exalted plane. If not, existence would become unbearable. Activity and industry merged with increased spiritual insight form a union that may preserve life beyond the normal limits.

Life on a higher plane than comfort and ease may seem strange in our culture, but it is an important quality of men who survive. This point has grave consequences for the comfort-oriented man lost in the wilderness. In Utah a man once died of dehydration beside a desert stream because the water was uncomfortably dirty.

Time is life, and where existence is reduced to a hand-to-mouth level, comfort must take a second seat. In survival terms we might say that comfort only gets in the way. In a literal sense a strong man may die of exposure if he neglects himself, but he may also die if he babies himself.

Lessons of survival learned in a classroom or laboratory setting may be helpful, but they will never replace direct application. My own experience has taught me that it is possible to rise above the comfort-seeking level in a primitive situation and establish priorities which not only insure my survival but grant me the added qualities of confidence and serenity as I attempt to exist in my environment. Even when the going gets rough and death becomes a grim possibility, that confidence and serenity never leave; thus struggles become challenges and my mind is better able to function without fear or panic.

I am reminded of the man who, alone in a vast desert with no hat, no water, and a broken leg, pulled himself up on one bruised and battered elbow and smiled at a bunch of dry grass, saying, "You know, if this keeps up I *might* get discouraged."

Through the Department of Youth Leadership at Brigham Young University I have presented the challenge of primitive survival to several thousand students. Under some of the toughest wilderness conditions these students have tramped hundreds of miles across rivers, mountains, and deserts of the West. There is no question in my mind that young people today are as tough as their pioneer forefathers. However, the most disturbing discovery of these expeditions has been the types of stress that cause people to give up. Many students drop in their tracks, not from physical exhaustion, but from mental anguish. They are often afraid to make the effort once the challenge is realized.

Then there is the other extreme—those who at first appearance seem not to be able to make it but who plow through to the end despite their physical limitations. They have their minds set on success. Incidents from two expeditions illustrate this positive stubbornness in a survival situation.

John was overweight and a slow hiker. He found the pace exhausting and breathing difficult in the intense heat of the desert. Water was scarce and the small group of students was bent on pushing to a small seep spring some twenty miles away. Worried, I assigned two students to hang back and keep an eye on him. Two instructors, in good shape, pushed ahead, running, with instructions to bring back water for the stragglers.

At the seep spring, several hours later, I was surprised to hear that John had made it completely on his own. To top it off, he had assisted one of the students assigned to him in bringing in another student who had a sprained ankle. They came in singing.

During the weeks that followed, John became the physician of his group and spent hours helping others. He made the 300-mile trek and never required more than his share of the meager food and water.

On another expedition, we had been three weeks on the trail, our destination taking us into the wind, which was blowing in the first winter storm. The terrain was steep and broken. The advance scout returned with word of a large overhanging cliff which would shelter the whole group until the storm passed. It was located about eight miles away near the top of a high ridge, and we began heading for it just as the sun went down.

We had been several days on meager rations and water, and many of the students had bad blisters which were par for any course of this kind. Our food supply consisted of a bag of flour and some Brigham brush (*Ephedra*) for making a warm drink.

The first group to reach the cave built a fire and rolled up in blankets to sleep, too worn out to eat. A short time later three more exhausted students came in with word that six others were having a rough time about three miles from the cave, halfway up the steep hill. The rest of the students were struggling up in small groups.

By this time it was dark, the wind had increased to a gale, and snow was falling. I found the group at the cave arguing with the three who had brought in the report. The three wanted the others to help make Brigham tea and ash cakes (flour and water patted into small cakes and baked in hot ashes) to take back to the struggling students below. The arguing proved futile, so the three alone prepared about fifty ash cakes and warm Brigham drink. Then one stayed at the fire cooking more food while the other two went back down the mountain with food and drink to aid the six laggers.

By two o'clock a.m. they had brought in the last of the men, fed them again, and stacked up a huge pile of firewood. They warmed cold feet, doctored blisters, and cheered hearts as best they could under the circumstances. These men I made my leaders.

**2**

Fig. 6. Makeshift shelter for wind protection

# SHELTER

One of the first skills a survivalist must learn is how to construct a shelter. He must also know what type of shelter is most appropriate for a given situation and that the techniques used for building it depend upon need and time. Most shelters should be built according to a few basic specifications; however, special circumstances such as rain or snowstorms or extremely cold weather may dictate any kind of makeshift protection which can be built in a hurry (Fig. 6). Nevertheless, after a degree of comfort has been achieved, a semipermanent shelter should be constructed to assure safety in the event conditions get worse.

Building for survival requires more than a minimum of effort and calls for sound planning. Most essential to this planning is the selection of a campsite. A good campsite provides:

- Protection from wind and storms
- Protection from flash floods, rock falls, high tides

- Freedom from poisonous plants, insect pests (ants, mosquitoes, fleas), and harmful animals
- Level ground for a bed and a fireplace
- Availability of materials for making a shelter and a bed
- An inexhaustible source of firewood
- Food sources and drinking water
- Dry ground located away from creek bottoms and green grassy areas

A good fire pit is also essential to survival. As it is used primarily for heating and cooking, it should be:

- At least eight inches deep and lined with stones
- Surrounded with spark protectors, which can be made from green pine boughs or upright sticks (If the protectors are placed at least six inches high, most popping sparks will be stopped.)
- Located in a direct line with the shelter entrance and slightly forward from the center, as this allows ample space at the back of the lodge

Also of major importance in building for survival are the dimensions and strength of the shelter. It must:

- Allow free movement around the fire
- Provide space for a dry woodpile just inside the opening
- Provide plenty of storage space for food and gear
- Allow for a fair-sized fire pit for cooking and heating and enough space from walls and ceiling to prevent flames and sparks from catching in thatch materials
- Be strong enough to withstand high winds and heavy snowfalls (Figs. 7 and 8) (There is nothing

Fig. 7. Framework for large shelter

Fig. 8. Heavy thatching for sturdy shelter

quite like having your shelter fall in on you at 3:00 a.m.) Its construction should include:

• Strong supporting poles lashed firmly, although most other poles and thatching can be laid on without lashing
• Heavy branches stacked against the finished lodge to prevent the wind from scattering the thatching when it is composed of grass and boughs
• Plenty of matting and grass for a floor covering, which must be kept at least one foot away from the fire and stirred up each evening or, even better, removed completely from the shelter and then respread—especially important in snake country

## Lean-to

Easy-to-build windbreaks serve well for summer living and give ample protection in cold weather if sturdy (Fig. 9). However, they are only temporary emergency

**Fig. 9. Three-sided lean-to**

shelters. When constructed, a lean-to should provide protection from the prevailing *night* wind, contain a large reflector so that maximum heat can be obtained from the fire, and be three-sided so that maximum protection can be obtained.

## Wickiup

A good wickiup takes only a little longer to build than a lean-to and is much more serviceable (Fig. 10). This comfortable dwelling is one of the best, as it provides protection from all sides. It consists of a tripod on which a tight circle of poles is stacked to form a large tepee or cone-shaped frame. Over this frame is placed a thatching of grass, leaves, reeds, bark, rotten wood, pine boughs, and even dirt. The entrance can be large and face the rising sun, or it can be small and provide protection from all outside breezes. One can make the floor space fourteen feet across, if he uses twenty-foot poles, and provide sleeping space for eight (Fig. 11).

**Fig. 10. Wickiup**
**Fig. 11. Large wickiup**

Fig. 12. Rock shelter (cave)

## Rock

The favorite natural protection of the Indian people in the West was the rock shelter, an overhanging cliff or bank that affords protection from the elements (Fig. 12). With a minimum of effort these shallow caves can be turned into first-class living quarters.

In the winter, rock shelters facing south catch the sun's warmth most of the day. For added protection low windbreaks or reflectors can be built across the front of the cave. Poles leaned against the outside edge of the roof and thatching, as in the construction of a wickiup, constitute a cave shelter that can be completely sealed from the elements.

## Insulated Wattlework

A little more time and patience is needed in the construction of a wattlework shelter, but the comfort it provides is worth the extra effort (Fig. 13). Each wall

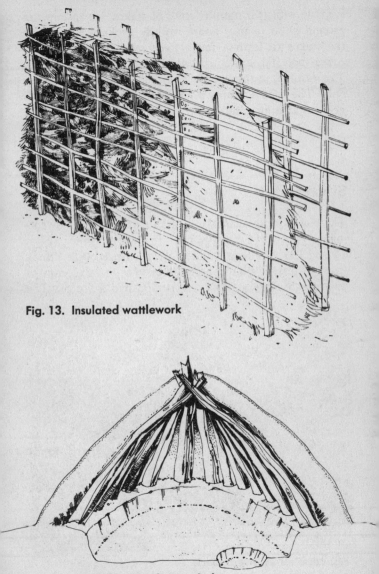

Fig. 13. Insulated wattlework

Fig. 14. Cross section of sweat lodge

is made with two parallel rows of stakes driven into the ground about a foot apart, willow sticks woven along the stakes to form a fairly tight mesh, and grass and other material stuffed between the two woven walls. The result is a thick, insulated wall that will stop any cold. The roof is simply made of poles and willows with grass thatching piled on top. Heavy willow rods and brush are piled on top of the grass to keep the wind from blowing it away.

## Sweat Lodge

The Navajo Indians make a small earth lodge for sweating purposes, but it also serves as a warm shelter (Figs. 14 and 15). Simply a small wickiup covered with a thick layer of dirt, it should be built over a pit large enough to accommodate at least one person and a fire pit. The

Fig. 15. Finished sweat lodge

earthen covering should seal off all areas where air might enter. The entrance must be small, large enough only for a person to crawl into, and should have as tight a covering as possible.

For warming this shelter a large fire must be built outside the entrance and several rocks heated. A small pit dug inside and to the left of the entrance serves as the heating pit. A person sitting inside can reach out through the entrance with a set of wooden tongs, pick a hot rock out of the fire, and pull it in, making sure that all the sparks and coals are shaken off. A single rock in the pit will heat the shelter for several hours. When it begins to cool, it can be replaced by another rock from the hot bed of coals outside.

## Snow

Snow caves are the simplest to construct, as they are merely dug into a snowbank that has a good crust, but they are not generally warm (Figs. 16 and 17). If well built, however, snow shelters can be heated adequately; but if they are to be comfortable, a lot of matting and floor covering are necessary. Lean-to shelters and wicki-ups covered with snow are excellent.

## Matting and Bedding

Sleeping in some degree of comfort is also an important part of the shelter and can be achieved rather easily. Dry grass, pine boughs, sagebrush bark, cattail stalks, bulrushes, and reeds make excellent bedding, and can be found at any time of the year. In the winter, dry grass is located at the base of cliffs that face the south. Snow usually melts away in these areas and the sun

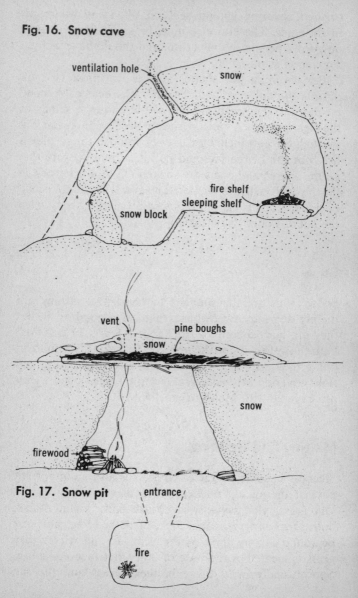

**Fig. 16. Snow cave**

ventilation hole

snow

fire shelf
sleeping shelf

snow block

vent    pine boughs

snow

snow

firewood

**Fig. 17. Snow pit**    entrance

fire

keeps the grass dry. Rats nests that contain enough grass for bedding are usually found in cracks and small caves.

## Hot Coal Bed

Heated ground under a bed makes even the coldest nights comfortable. But care should be taken not to

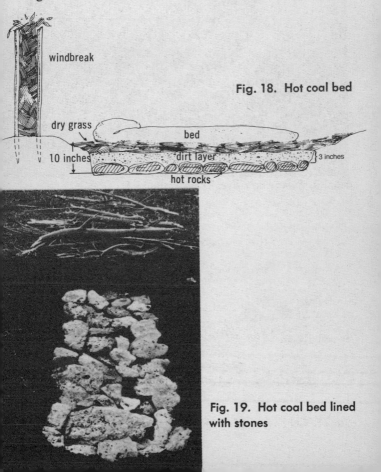

windbreak

Fig. 18. Hot coal bed

dry grass

bed

10 inches

dirt layer

3 inches

hot rocks

Fig. 19. Hot coal bed lined with stones

allow direct contact with the hot stones. Even after several hours of cooling, the rocks will still burn holes in bedding. After the stones are heated by a fire built right in the pit, the ashes which have accumulated are scraped out before the covering of dirt is applied (Figs. 18-20).

Fig. 20. Removing ashes from heated bed

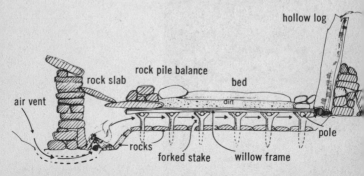

Fig. 21. Chimney draft bed

## Chimney Draft Bed

The construction of this type of bed is a complicated challenge for the good survivalist, but once built, it is unequaled for comfort in cold weather (Fig. 21). Such a bed is best constructed inside a large shelter or cave since the bed itself provides very little protection from wind and storm.

**3**

Fig. 22. Starting a fire with the bow drill

# FIRE

The importance of a good fire can hardly be underestimated. Even in warm weather a fire is essential, not only for warmth at night but for cooking, signaling, purifying water, and aiding in the manufacture of various useful items. The following methods are exhaustive and should be studied carefully. Reading about how to start a fire without matches is one thing, but doing it another.

An inexperienced person in the wilds without matches or other modern methods of making fire will find that primitive methods are beyond his ability. On the other hand, an experienced artisan may create a good fire in a matter of seconds, using only materials found in nature (Fig. 22).

Success in making fires is achieved only with practice and carefully wrought equipment. No amount of effort will produce a fire when dexterity is lacking and when equipment is crude. Getting that first spark to burst into flame is somewhat of a surprise, but from that moment, it is almost certain that future attempts will be successful.

## Tinder

Tinder is made from dry bark which is light and fluffy and from shredded grass, dry moss, birds nests, and various plant fibers.

The preparation of tinder requires special attention. It should always be finely shredded (but not powdered) so that the bundle is a soft, fluffy, fibrous mass which will not fall apart. Rubbing the bundle between the hands is perhaps the best way to make tinder light and fluffy (Fig. 23).

Fig. 23. Preparing tinder

The following list contains the more common tinders available in nature. Others may be found by experimentation in different geographical areas. (The drawings in the Appendix will help you identify many of these trees and plants.)

## Barks

- Cliffrose (*Cowania*): shrub—outer bark from trunk and larger limbs

- Cottonwood (*Populus*): tree—inner cambium layer on old dead trees
- Sagebrush (*Artemisia tridentata*): shrub—outer bark from trunk of larger plants
- Juniper (*Juniperus*): tree—outer bark from trunk of mature trees

## Plant Fibers and Silks

- Yucca (*Yucca*): fibers from pounded dead leaves or ready-made at the base of dead plants
- Nettle (*Urtica*): fibers from pounded dead stalks
- Milkweed (*Asclepias*): fibers from pounded dead stalks; also silk from pods
- Dogbane (*Apocynum*): fibers from pounded dead stalks
- Thistle (*Cirsium*): down from tops
- Cattail (*Typha*): down from seed heads
- Various grasses: dead leaf blades, partially decomposed, lying at base of plants

# Flint and Steel

Steel, a luxury item, is rarely found in nature and then only if someone has left or lost it. When present in the form of a pocketknife, nail file, and so forth, it can be used in combination with a hard stone to produce sparks hot enough to catch tinder.

Flint stones come in a wide range of types, all of which contain some silica. Agate, jasper, and quartzite are perhaps the best, though any silica stone will do. It should be broken into angular chunks to produce sharp edges.

The tinder bundle must be of the finest quality ma-

**Fig. 24. Making a nest in a tinder bundle**

terial, sagebrush, cottonwood, or cliffrose bark being the best. A small nest is made in the tinder bundle and the finest shredded material is loosely sprinkled in the depression (Fig. 24).

Striking the spark takes a little practice. The best method is for a person to hold the stone in one hand and the closed blade of a pocketknife, or something similar, in the other, and with a rather loose-jointed-wrist approach, strike the sharp edge of the stone rather severely until sparks fly off and fall onto the tinder bundle (Fig. 25). A thin wisp of smoke will signal that one has caught. Then the tinder bundle must be picked up quickly and very gently, and the spark must be blown on with short puffs of air. If the timing of these actions is just right, the spark will spread and burst into flame (Fig. 26).

A more sure way of getting sparks to hold is to use specially prepared charred tinder. Once a fire has been produced by other means, it is a simple matter to make plenty of charred tinder for quick, easy fires later on.

Fig. 25. Striking a spark

Fig. 26. Blowing a spark into flame

Manure, wood punk, or pithy plant stalks are burned until very black and then smothered in an airtight container or simply stepped on several times in very dry dust. Plant stalks should be split to expose the pith. When charred, the material can be stored in small containers or wrapped inside tinder bundles until time for use. For best results manure, punk, and pith, after charring, should be crumbled into powder.

A handkerchief, a piece of cloth cut from a shirttail, or a piece of cotton charred in the same manner is even superior to punk or pith, if it can be sacrificed. The charred material, placed in the tinder bundle, catches readily when sparks fall on it and holds longer than punk or pith. Sources of excellent charred tinder materials are:

- Masses of very soft dry rot found in the dry rotted, fallen logs of the cottonwood tree (*Populus*) and some other trees
- A pithy core of superior quality found in the center stalk or spike of the yucca (*Yucca*)
- An excellent pithy core found in the stalks of the mullein (*Verbascum*)
- A large but rather tough pith found in the stalks of the elderberry (*Sambucus*)
- A soft pith found in the stalks of the sunflower (*Helianthus*)
- Manure: dried chunks found in ample supply in most areas frequented by game and livestock

## Bow Drill

Making fire with a bow drill is a simple matter if the apparatus is constructed correctly. It has four parts: a fireboard, a drill, a socket, and a bow (Fig. 27).

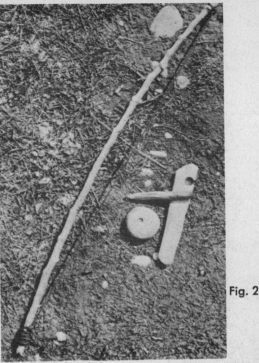

Fig. 27. Bow drill

An excellent fireboard, which should be about ½ inch thick, can be made from a dead cottonwood branch. A slight depression must be drilled along one edge and can be smoothed and deepened by a few turns of the bow and drill. A notch, which reaches to the center of the pit, is cut in the side of the board and catches the fine powder ground off by the drill. It is in this fine powder that the spark is formed (Figs. 28 and 29).

The drill may be of the same wood as the fireboard and should be from 8 to 12 inches long and about ¾ of an inch in diameter. The top end is sharpened to a point while the bottom is blunt.

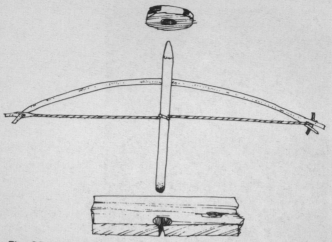

Fig. 28. Bow drill

Fig. 29. The all-important notch

The socket is made by drilling a depression in any piece of hardwood or stone that fits the hand. When in use, the drill runs smoother if the socket is lubricated with grease. Enough lubrication can be obtained by rubbing the top of the drill stick through the hair or on each side of the nose. The use of water for lubricating a socket only makes it swell and bind.

The bow should be 18 to 25 inches long and about ½ inch in diameter. A branch with a fork on one end makes an excellent bow. The best string is a strip of ¼-inch-wide buckskin or other leather, but substitutes can be made from plant fibers, shoelaces, or some other cord. The cord is attached to one end of the bow and twisted until it is tight and round before being tied to the other end. It is a good idea to fix one end in such a way that it may be loosened or tightened as needed. If the bow drill does not run smoothly, it may be that a little more twist in the cord is needed.

In using the bow drill, one places the fireboard on a flat piece of bark or wood. The spark will fall onto this piece and can then be carried to the tinder. Another method involves the digging of a small depression under the fireboard. The tinder is placed in the hole under the board in a position which allows the spark to fall directly into it. The proper position for working the set calls for a person to get down on one knee and place one foot on the fireboard to hold it steady. He then places the drill, with the bow cord twisted once around it, in the fireboard socket. Using the hand socket to apply pressure, he then moves the bow back and forth in a sawing motion with steady, even strokes until the drill tip is smoking well (Fig. 30). He gradually spins the drill faster and applies more pressure with the hand socket. After a lot of black dust from the drill starts collecting beside the notch and there is plenty of smoke, there should be enough heat for a spark. The drill is then

Fig. 30. Getting a spark

Fig. 31. Lifting the drill from the socket

Fig. 32.  Placing the spark in tinder

Fig. 33.  Blowing the spark into flame

carefully lifted away, and the pile of black dust is lightly fanned with the hand. If there is a spark, the pile will begin to glow. When this happens the spark must be quickly but carefully placed in the tinder and blown into flame (Figs. 31-33).

## Hand Drill

The basic principle for making a fire with a hand drill is the same as that for making one with the bow drill. However, instead of using a bow and socket, the drill is simply twirled between the palms of the hands. The hands should be arched out stiffly for the best results, and the drill should be at least 16 inches long and tapered slightly from the bottom toward the top. Since this method is so difficult, it is not recommended as a sure way to get fire. Aborigines seem to have the skill necessary for this operation, but few so-called civilized people ever achieve it even after much practice.

Fig. 34. Using the hand drill

This method is speeded up when two people work together. One person spins until his hands reach the bottom of the spindle and then the other takes over at the top. In this way the spinning motion is constant (Fig. 34).

## Other Methods

Various other less satisfactory techniques used to make fires include the fire saw, in which two sticks are rubbed together in a notch until a spark is formed; the fire thong, in which a strong vine or rope is pulled back and forth in a split stick; and optics, in which a lens from glasses, a flashlight, field glasses, the bottom of a pop bottle, or a bottle filled with water is used to concentrate the rays of the sun.

## Maintaining a Fire

Once a fire is made, a person may need to take certain precautions to keep it going. When he camps in one spot for a period of time, he can keep a fire alive through the night by building up a deep bed of hot coals and banking them with ashes and a thin layer of dirt. The important thing is to keep the wind from the coals.

Tinder can be prepared for traveling purposes from shredded bark which is baked until it is powder dry. It can then be carried in a dry container or wrapped in several strips of bark. The Piute Indians ingeniously transported live fires over long distances by simply making a long bundle out of a core of shredded sagebrush or other bark placed on several thicknesses of dry stripped bark. Additional layers were placed on top and the whole bundle was wrapped tightly with more

**Fig. 35. Fire bundles (the top has been burning 6 hours)**

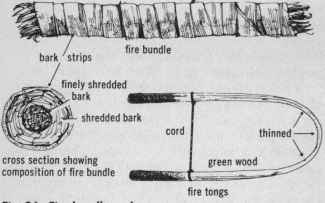

bark strips

fire bundle

finely shredded bark

shredded bark

cross section showing composition of fire bundle

cord

thinned

green wood

fire tongs

**Fig. 36. Fire bundle and tongs**

strips of bark. When finished, the fire-carrier looked like a giant cigar about two feet long and six inches in diameter (Figs. 35 and 36). A hot coal was placed in one end and the Indian traveled with the fire carrier in his hand or stuck in his belt. Such a bundle would hold a live spark from six to twelve hours. Usually two or three bundles were made and carried. When one burned low, the Indian stopped and built a small fire, and in a few minutes he had a new supply of hot coals from which he would light another bundle.

## Miscellaneous Hints

- A fire blower for stirring up dead fires can be made from any hollow stem. Canary reed grass and elderberry stems are excellent.
- Flames should be used for boiling and baking and coals for broiling and frying.
- Split wood burns better than whole chunks or logs.
- A log will burn in two; therefore, there is no need to chop it.
- Soft woods give more light than hard woods.
- Reflectors should be used for warmth.
- Fire tongs save scorched fingers.

**4**

Fig. 37. Water pockets—an easy-to-locate source of water

# WATER

The Mountain West is often the scene of tragic experiences involving lack of water. But with a little luck and training anyone should be able to provide himself with enough drinking water to stay alive. There are areas, however, that require special equipment if water is to be secured, for much of the desert area of the Great Basin is devoid of running water. Sources can be located without too much trouble if a person knows how to look for them (Fig. 37).

Most of the moisture can be found on the sloping side of the hills in an area of dry mountain ranges. The other side is usually a steep escarpment and has faster runoff and less ground area for the collection of water. Narrow canyons and gullies should be followed up to their heads because small seeps and springs are often located nearby and run only a short distance before drying up.

The water table is usually close to the surface and one can locate it by digging:

- At the base of cliffs and rocks where an abnormal amount of vegetation is thriving

Fig. 38. Drinking from a pool of water

Fig. 39. Selecting a site to dig for water

- In dry mudholes, sinks, riverbeds, and the bends of riverbeds, the latter usually providing the easiest source of water
- At the base of large sand dunes on the shady or steep sides
- Anywhere the ground is damp or muddy
- In low spots where patches of salt grass, cattails, greasewood, willows, or elderberries grow (Figs. 38 and 39)

Ore dumps and tailings indicate that water might be nearby in old mine shafts and pits.

## Getting Water from the Soil

Obtaining water from the soil involves a few techniques with which a person who is going into the wilds should acquaint himself:

- A hole dug in damp or muddy sink areas allows water to seep in and collect (Fig. 40).
- Mud wrung in a shirt or other cloth will force out water.

Fig. 40. Finding water at a depth of 10 inches

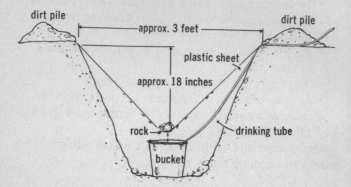

**Fig. 41. Cross section of an evaporation still**

An evaporation still—a new invention developed by two American scientists, Dr. Ray D. Jackson and Dr. Cornelius H. M. van Bavel of the U.S. Department of Agriculture—involves some special equipment but is simple to construct (Fig. 41). A sheet of 6-by-6 foot clear plastic, a plastic drinking tube, and a container are all that are needed and can be included in a survival kit. A drinking tube is attached to the container—usually a bucket—and the bucket is placed into a 3-foot hole. Then a plastic sheet is stretched over the hole and held in place with dirt, which seals the hole off from the outside air. Next a rock is placed in the center of the plastic to weight it down until it comes to within about 2 inches of the bucket. The drinking tube, fastened in the bucket, is arranged so that it extends outside the still.

Two of these stills in operation in even the driest deserts will produce enough water daily for one person. Green plants and sliced cactus placed in the pit will increase the amount of

water. It is best to place the still in old riverbeds
and in deep rich soil at the bottoms of gullies
where moisture is most plentiful.

## Collecting Water from the Air and from Plants

In many arid regions of the world primitive peoples supply themselves with water by arising before dawn to
mop up the dew from rocks and plants. A person using
this technique in desert areas can find a large supply of
dew in the early morning (Fig. 42).

The easiest way to gather it is to use a handkerchief
or a shirt to gently mop it up and then wring it into a
container. If a handkerchief or other cloth is not available, a handful of dry grass will do the job. It is possible
to mop up almost a quart an hour using this method.

Many plants and trees contain enough water to allay

Fig. 42. Dew available in early morning

thirst, but getting it is a problem. A cactus can be cut and peeled and the moisture sucked out, but this is not the same as drinking running water; it is more like drinking Elmer's glue. However, large cacti in the Southwest can be a good source of water when the tops are cut off and the center pulp mashed and stirred with a stick. The pulp can then be wrung to obtain the water.

## Collecting Water from Water Pockets

In the Southwest much of the desert is made up of up-lifted sandstone ridges or folds that sometimes run a hundred miles or more and completely dissect the land areas into separate valleys and drainages (Fig. 43).

Fig. 43. Ridges and valleys cut into sandstone by water runoff

Fig. 44. Narrow canyons—source of water pockets

These exposed areas of stone absorb very little moisture, and a light rainstorm or snowstorm can cause considerable runoff which in turn cuts deep channels and scoops out pockets in the surface. These pockets are numerous but extremely difficult to find, and as a result a person must ignore his basic instinct which causes him to look in the lower parts of a valley for water and instead seek the high ground where the water pockets are located. The areas which one should carefully check are side canyons, narrow clefts, and especially white sandstone ridges (Fig. 44).

These hidden pockets may hold water for several months after a rain. In fact, some pockets are actually

Fig. 45. Water pockets formed in sandstone

large tanks holding hundreds of gallons, while others are very small, holding only a few quarts (Fig. 45).

I have traveled with survival students as far as 200 miles on foot across southwestern deserts without a canteen, relying mostly on these water pockets and a few small springs and seeps. Some stretches, to be sure, were completely devoid of water, but by carefully studying the terrain and sandstone formations, we have always been able to prepare a route and cross these areas to water-pocket country on the other side.

## Precautions in Using Water

A person inexperienced in the outdoors will want to be thrifty in his use of water and will benefit from a few precautions suggested here:

- Nothing should be eaten if water is not available —eating uses up the body's water reserve.
- Water should be stored in the stomach and not in a canteen; people have died from dehydration with water still in their canteens.
- Water polluted by animals or mud tastes bad, but it is harmless if boiled.
- Muddy water can be partially cleared by allowing it to stand overnight, run through several thicknesses of cloth or a grass filter, or seep through the bank into a hole dug about a foot away. If the water is brackish or salty the top six inches of salty soil between the hole and the source of water should be removed before the water is allowed to seep into the hole.
- There should be no traveling during the heat of the day and walking should be done slowly, not in a hurry.
- Such things as pebbles in the mouth, small sips of water, and chewing gum may relieve thirst, but they do not stop dehydration.
- The drinking of blood or urine only increases dehydration of the body. But it helps to soak clothing in urine, as it cools the body during the evaporation process.

**5**

Fig. 46. Grinding sunflower seeds on a metate

# PLANTS

The American West is certainly no Garden of Eden with respect to food plants but the variety offered is extensive enough, and anyone with a good understanding of harvesting and preparation methods can live off these plant resources (Fig. 46).

It has been said that a person who can survive on the Great Plains can survive anywhere in the world. There are areas that surpass the hot barrenness of the Sahara, the cold ruggedness of Mongolia, and the jagged steepness of the Alps. But in all of these conditions nature has provided adequately for the trained survivalist. The food quest is exacting and strenuous, and knowledge of the plant life is a must, inasmuch as so many edible species resemble poisonous ones. A careful study of these plants is perhaps the most important phase of outdoor training.

Moreover, the survivalist must be aware of the impact that one man can have on a wildland environment, especially on pristine desert lands. Some plants take several years to grow large enough to harvest, and one meal could require several plants, perhaps the number found in about an acre of land. For example, some plants are becoming rare as their habitats are being destroyed by agriculture and urbanization. One person could easily gather all the sego lily bulbs that occur in an acre or two of natural grassland for only one meal. Plants that have an annual crop of edible parts that can be harvested without injury to the plant should be used first. In other words, the survivalist should exercise his "ecological conscience" and conserve whenever possible.

A certain amount of taste-bud training, which comes from experimentation and mental determination, is often necessary if one is to find some of the plants palatable. One should taste wild foods often and do so with a positive attitude. Many people die amid plenty simply because they cannot "stomach" wild foods; however, in these cases the stomach reacts only to the stimulus given by a prejudiced brain—some people even develop defense mechanisms against eating certain foods. Needless to say, these defenses can kill even a healthy person lost in the wilds.

## Harvesting Food Plants

### Roots

Finding an edible root is fairly easy, but most roots grow deep, and digging them out can be difficult unless one is prepared with a few good techniques. Skillfully applied, a simple device called a digging stick saves time and energy that is otherwise expended scraping and grubbing with flat stones and fingers (Fig. 47). The stick is made from a stave of hardwood about three feet long and one inch in diameter. After the bark is removed the stick is hardened in the fire and the tip of it rubbed into a chisel shape on a coarse rock. Green wood hardens

**Fig. 47. Digging wild onions with a digging stick**

**Fig. 48. Proper use of digging stick**

after about four or five scorchings in the fire, but several scorchings are required to drive out the sap. Care must be taken that the wood does not burn, for a good fire-hardened stick must be baked, not charred.

Digging down to a tasty root involves moving a lot of dirt, and the digger finds that it is easier if he makes the root come to him. He can do this by pushing the stick down alongside the plant until it is even with or below the root. Then by slightly prying, but mostly by lifting, he can flip the root to the surface (Fig. 48).

## Seeds

When seeds are ripe they can be gathered in large quantities with a seed beater and a gathering basket. The seed beater is a small woven dish or ladle used to knock the ripened seeds from the plants. It should be dish-shaped so that it can catch and propel the seeds into the

Fig. 49. Rubbing seeds from plant

basket. The basket must be large enough to catch the
seeds yet small enough to be held in one arm. A shallow
woven tray is ideal, but a shirt held open with a willow
hoop will also work.

Plants that form large amounts of seeds in clusters
such as Amaranth (*Amaranthus*) need only be stripped
with the hand for removal of the seeds. Flower seeds
such as those of the nutritious sunflower (*Helianthus*)
can be beaten from the head with a seed beater and
also picked by hand or rubbed from the head on a flat
stone (Fig. 49).

## Preparing Food Plants

### Roots

Flour from roots can be made by drying and grinding
the roots on a metate in much the same manner as that
used for seeds. A metate is a slab of rock that has been
smoothed by erosion (see p. 74). Roots may be roasted
whole and eaten like baked potatoes or mashed on a
metate and eaten like mashed potatoes. Roasting, baking, or boiling may be used for most roots unless leaching is necessary. Leaching of bitter greens, roots, and
nuts is done by boiling them in several changes of water
or by pouring water through a bag of the mashed food.
However, this process takes away much of the food
value of plants and should be used only when the food
is too bitter to be eaten otherwise.

A steaming pit is the most effective way to cook roots
and greens, as well as meat and other foods. The pit is
lined with stones and a fire is built in it. After about an
hour the coals are scraped out and the pit is lined with
wet green grass. The food is then placed on the grass
and covered quickly with more wet grass. Next, water is
poured on the food to induce steam, and the pit and its

**Fig. 50. Lining a steaming pit with stones**

contents are quickly covered with flat rocks or a piece of cloth, canvas, or hide. Dirt is then heaped over the entire pit to seal in the steam, and the food is allowed to cook in the pit for several hours. One advantage of preparing food in this manner is that its flavor and nutritional value are saved (Figs. 50-52).

Roots and berries can be dried for future use. The roots are cooked and mashed into small flat cakes and then dried on flat rocks until hard. Berries must be partially dried first and then mashed into cakes for the

Fig. 51. Preparing the pit for grass and food

Fig. 52. Applying a dirt covering to the pit

final drying by being pounded in a mortar or they can be mixed with pounded meat for pemmican. However, these dried cakes must be broken up or ground before they are added to stew.

## Seeds

Seeds must be threshed and winnowed if most of the chaff and stems are to be removed. One can accomplish this by beating the seeds with sticks and then tossing

them on a winnowing tray, letting the wind blow away
the chaff. This ancient method may seem rather crude,
but it is effective under limited conditions. Seeds may
also be tossed in a blanket or tossed into the air from a
pile on the ground. A blanket or tray saves many of the
tossed seeds from being lost in the dirt. One can win-
now small amounts by taking a handful at a time and
blowing away the chaff while he pours the seeds from
one hand to the other (Figs. 53-55).

Most seeds are tastier and more nutritious when
ground into flour or cracked for mush than when eaten
whole. A most valuable method of making flour or
cracking seeds involves a grinding stone. A handful of
dry seeds is placed on a smooth stone (the metate) and
ground with a mano or handstone (a loaf-shaped rock
with one flat side). The handstone is held in the hands
and rubbed back and forth on the metate with a pounding, scraping motion. It is best to work with the metate
placed in the middle of a blanket to avoid losing seeds
during the grinding process. Wet grinding may prove

Fig. 53. Beating seeds

Fig. 54. Winnowing seeds    Fig. 55. Winnowing seeds by
by tossing                                    handfuls

easier for some and is accomplished by dampening the seeds until they are soft and then grinding them into a dry paste (Fig. 56).

Seeds may also be dried or parched for preservation. The parching process is not difficult but requires a steady hand and a good parching tray. A tray can be made from willows woven closely to form a large shallow bowl. A dishpan will also do. The bottom of the tray is covered with seeds and then a layer of hot hardwood coals is poured into it. The contents are stirred and the tray is shaken until all of the seeds are toasted.

**Fig. 56. Using a metate to grind seeds**

The hot coals are then flipped away while the contents of the tray are poured onto a flat rock.

Dried seeds, roots, and berries can be safely stored in pits at the back of dry rock shelters and in crevices. A pit approximately two feet deep and lined with grass is sufficient. The dried food is placed in the pit and covered with dry sagebrush leaves and juniper bark, and

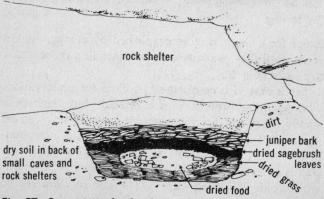

rock shelter

dirt

juniper bark

dried sagebrush leaves

dried grass

dry soil in back of small caves and rock shelters

dried food

**Fig. 57. Storage pit for food**

then at least six inches of dirt is piled over all of this (Fig. 57). A pit made in dry dust and soil beneath an overhanging ledge will remain dry for years, and insects and rodents will rarely bother it.

## Barks and Greens

Barks, leaves, and stems should be stripped and picked with care, and only the young tender portions should be selected. If possible, one should keep them fresh and cool while gathering them, but they must not be soaked in water to be kept fresh.

## Edible Plants*

The following list contains many of the more important food plants found in the Great Basin plateau areas of the western United States. In this rugged section of America the plant life is rather restricted and in most cases adapted to arid conditions. The higher elevations produce a wider variety of edible species which also grow in the desert valleys along stream courses. Edible seeds are the most common food source and comprise over half of the available species. I have supplied the location for only those plants that grow in definite habitats. My intent is not to differentiate between native and introduced plants—if a plant grows in uncultivated areas, for my purposes here it is considered wild.

**Note:** In the following list of edible plants, the common name(s) is listed first, followed by the scientific—generic and species—name(s). Whenever the generic

* Some plants which are edible are also poisonous unless prepared with caution; others are easily confused with poisonous plants. To aid the reader and to caution him, a † precedes each of these plants.

term (always capitalized and italicized) appears alone, usually many—and in some cases all—species of that genus are edible, but are too numerous to list. Whenever the species name (italicized, but not capitalized) is listed after the generic term, only that species is to be used. Each drawing in the Appendix for a given plant is of only one species, but is usually one of the most common species of the given genus and is often representative of it.

### Amaranth, Pigweed; *Amaranthus*

Description: Amaranth, an annual herb, has veiny alternate leaves and bears seeds which are black and grow in terminal or axillary clusters. (See p. 215.)

Preparation and Uses: Pigweed is known as America's forgotten cereal grain. Its shiny black seeds make a suitable cereal raw or cooked and may be added to soups, stews, and bread. The young leaves make a superior green when cooked like spinach soon after they are picked.

In late summer the seeds may be stripped from the stalk by hand or the whole plant can be pulled up. One can thresh the seeds by beating bundles of the stalks with a stick and winnowing the chaff as he tosses the contents in a blanket. The yield may amount to a pound or more of seeds from only a small armload of the plants.

### Arrowhead, Wappato; *Sagittaria latifolia*

Description: Arrowhead grows in water or marshes and is easily identified by its deep green arrowhead-shaped leaves that protrude from the water or lie flat like a lily pad. The stalk is a single stem that bears fruit which grows from lateral spikes in the form of round heads containing flat seeds. The fibrous root system spreads directly from the tuft of the leaves and grows some distance into the shallow mud. In the late fall small tubers form on the rootstalks. (See p. 215.)

Preparation and Uses: The small tubers, forming only in the late fall, can be gathered throughout the fall, winter, and early spring. One can harvest them by wading into the water and feeling in the mud with his toes or hands. He can often harvest large amounts by raking the water and mud to a depth of about six inches with a forked stick. This breaks the tubers from the roots so that they float to the surface. The only disadvantage to gathering arrowhead is that the weather is usually icy cold during the harvesting season and hence uncomfortable for the survivalist. In addition, he must be aware of conservation techniques; obviously an onslaught on streams or marshes will have a negative effect on the environment by unbalancing nature.

The tubers are roasted or baked to remove the stinging and poisonous properties and taste something like potatoes. They can be baked, mashed into cakes, and dried for future use.

### Arrowleaf Balsamroot, Balsamroot; *Balsamorrhiza*

Description: A member of the composite family, arrowleaf balsamroot is low growing and has arrow-shaped basal leaves and stems topped with yellow flowers that resemble sunflowers. (See p. 215.)

Preparation and Uses: The large root is edible when cooked. Some roots can be eaten raw but are bitter. The best way to prepare them is to steam large quantities for twenty-four hours or more and then mash and shape them into cakes for storage.

## Asparagus; *Asparagus officinalis*

Description: Asparagus grows in moist ground near civilization. Its young shoots rise from the ground in the early spring and later become tall and branching and bear red berries. (See p. 216.)

Preparation and Use: The young shoots can be eaten raw or cooked and prepared in the manner typical for domestic asparagus.

## Beeplant; *Cleome*

Description: Beeplants are annual herbs with stems that are one to three feet tall. The leaves are branching with three leaflets, and the seed pods are one to two inches in length. The flowers are yellow or rose-purple, depending on the species. These plants grow in sandy ground at lower elevations of the Southwest. (See p. 216.)

Preparation and Uses: The greens can be eaten if they are boiled in two or three changes of water to remove the bitter taste. However, they are tastier when mixed with other foods after they are cooked. The cooked shoots can be dried and used as an emergency food. After the plant is cooked for several hours, the liquid serves as a black dye.

## †Biscuit-root, Kouse; *Cymopterus*

Description: A member of the carrot family, biscuit-root consists of several edible species, having swollen bulblike roots. The plants grow on hillsides and in rocky places throughout the West and are often found in quite arid places. The flowers are borne on compound umbels and the leaves are divided into narrow segments like carrot leaves. Care should be taken not to confuse biscuit-root with related species that usually grow in damp areas and are often poisonous. This family should be studied carefully for identification of the various genera, some of which are deadly, such as the poison hemlock. (See p. 217.)

Preparation and Uses: The seeds of some species are edible when ground into mush or flour. The root is a favored ingredient of stews and tastes something like dumplings. It can be boiled or roasted in a pit for best results, and if mashed and dried in cakes after it is cooked, it will keep indefinitely. This was the famous "bread of cows" (kouse) so eagerly sought by Lewis and Clark.

## Blazing Star, Stickleaf; *Mentzelia*

Description: Blazing star is a coarse branching plant one to three feet tall, bearing beautiful yellow flowers and leaves covered with barbed hairs. Because of the barbed hairs the lance-shaped leaves often stick to clothing. The edges of the leaves are deeply cleft or pinnate. The root is buried deep as opposed to similar looking plants that have spreading root systems. Blazing star sometimes grows in seleniferous soils. (See p. 217.)

Preparation and Uses: The seeds, after they are parched and ground into flour or meal, can be used as a serviceable food for mush and bread.

## Bluegrass; *Poa* (Western)

Description: A grass common to rangeland, bluegrass bears seeds in narrow spreading seed heads. It is not too important to distinguish between the various grasses, as most that bear harvestable seeds in a grainlike husk are edible. (See p. 217.)

Preparation and Uses: The seeds, if harvested with a

seed beater, can be a good source of food when the season is right. But since most grass seeds drop shortly after maturity, the season is limited.

## †Bracken Fern; *Pteridium aquilinum*

Description: The most common of our ferns, bracken fern is coarse and covered with felty hairs at the base, and its young shoots uncurl in juicy stalks called fiddleheads (because of their resemblance in shape to the fiddle). The mature plant has a three-forked stem bearing light green fronds. (See p. 218.)

Preparation and Uses: Young fiddleheads have long been a popular potherb in many countries. They are best when cooked like asparagus or when eaten raw with other foods. The mature fern is tough and unpalatable and may be toxic if eaten in large quantities. Under ordinary conditions, one should not uproot the plant for food. The survivalist should also be aware that some people are sensitive to the mature leaves.

## Bristlegrass, Foxtail Millet; *Setaria*

Description: A grass with dense foxtail seed spikes which have long, stiff bristles, bristlegrass is a common species of wasteland and desert seeps. (See p. 218.)

Preparation and Uses: The grain of this plant is similar to wheat or millet and is easily obtained by parching to remove the husk. The seeds ground for flour or boiled for mush provide excellent nourishment.

## Buffaloberry; *Shepherdia argentea, S. canadensis*

Description: A shrub or small tree, buffaloberry is somewhat thorny with oval or nearly oval leaves. Its small red berries last late into the fall.

Preparation and Uses: The berries are edible and can be cooked in stews or dried and pounded for meal and pemmican. The taste of the summer berries may be strange to some palates, but they are not poisonous as many people have assumed.

## Bulrush; *Scirpus*

Description: Bulrush often grows taller than a man and has stems that are triangular in some species and round in others. A cluster of seeds grows at or near the tip. Bulrush grows along streams and marshes. (See p. 219.)

Preparation and Uses: The rootstalks are edible and should be peeled and boiled or eaten raw. The center core of the root is especially tasty. The young shoots just protruding from the mud are a delicacy raw or cooked, preferably raw. One harvests them by wading into the water and feeling down along the plant until he comes to the last shoot in a string of shoots that protrudes above the water. He pushes his hands into the mud until he finds the lateral rootstalk. By feeling along the rootstalk in a direction leading away from the last shoot, one can often find a protruding bulb from which the new shoot is starting. This is easily snapped off and is edible on the spot. When the only available water is brackish and unfit to drink, these young shoots will allay thirst for a long time.

The rootstalks, when peeled, dried, and pounded into flour, make a good bread. This flour can also be mixed with a flour made from the seeds of the same plant. These are harvested by stripping and winnowing and are an important source of grain food.

The slender stalks are generally too tough for eating, but they are useful as material for cordage, sandals, baskets, and mats.

## Burdock; *Arctium minus*

Description: Every farmer knows this bothersome weed. Burdock is characterized by large rhubarblike leaves and purple flowers that produce a soft burr. The leaves are often over ten inches wide and a foot long and are smooth and velvety to the touch. The burrs are characterized by a mass of slender hooked spines that are not stiff. They cling to clothes and socks but seldom prick the skin. (See pp. 219-20.)

Preparation and Uses: This useful plant has long been used in folk medicine for various external and internal complaints, generally as a tonic. The young leaves and shoots are edible when cooked as greens, and the root of the first-year plant is an excellent food when fried or roasted. If boiled, the root may be tough and strong unless the water is changed at least once.

The young stalks of the burdock can be peeled of their tough, bitter rind and the pithy center boiled for food. The roots can be dried and stored.

## Burreed; *Sparganium*

Description: Aquatic plants with branching, leafy stems, the burreeds have small round seed heads resembling a burr located on the sides and near the top of the stalks. (See p. 220.)

Preparation and Uses: The bulbous stem bases and tuberous roots of this plant are used for food in much the same way as cattails and bulrushes.

## †Camas; *Camassia*

Description: Camas, a member of the lily family growing in damp meadows, is characterized by grasslike slender leaves radiating from the base. The stem is usually one or two feet tall and topped with a spike of blue flowers. (See p. 221.) It should never be confused with the similar looking plant, death camas or *Zigadenus*, which is easily distinguished in appearance from camas by its smaller yellow or cream colored flowers. (See p. 221.) Careless identification has caused the death of wild plant eaters because the death camas is extremely poisonous. The common name, camas, should not be used as a guide to edibility, as *Veratrum* is also called camas and should be considered poisonous.

Camas should be harvested only when the plant is in bloom, for it is at this time that the survivalist can most easily distinguish it from the white or death camas. It can be harvested at other times of the year, but only by those who are very familiar with the plant's minute characteristics. It is possible after much observation of both plants to distinguish between them, both before and after flowering. Camas is never found growing in dry rocky ground as is the death camas; the flowers are blue, whereas the flowers of the death camas are smaller and yellow or cream colored; the leaf blades of most camas are slightly broader than those of most species of death camas; generally the bulbs of large mature camas are much larger than the largest bulbs of the death camas; camas grows mostly in the northern areas of the West: Idaho, Oregon, and Washington.

Preparation and Uses: The starchy bulb is an excellent food and can be gathered in large quantities with a digging stick. In meadows where these plants grow, a bushel of them can be gathered in just a few hours. The bulbs are best prepared by being baked in a pit oven. After they are cooked, they can be mashed and dried in cakes for storage. Camas bulbs were an important source of food to many early Indian tribes.

## Cattail; *Typha*

Description: Found along streams and marshes throughout the West, cattail has long bladelike leaves sometimes six feet long and a jointless stem terminating in a
sausage-shaped seed head. (See p. 221.)

Preparation and Uses: The cattail is an outstanding
edible plant. The roots, young shoots, seed heads, and
pollen are all edible, and the leaves make an excellent
material for weaving. The down from the head makes a
good insulation for blankets and sleeping bags.

The roots, when peeled and dried, can be made into
flour for bread. One can also obtain the starch from the
roots by mashing and soaking them in water and stirring
the mixture vigorously. After they have been stirred, the
roots should be allowed to sit overnight or until all the
starch settles to the bottom of the container. The water
is then poured off and the starch used as dough for making bread.

The young shoots are excellent when eaten raw or
boiled like asparagus. The centers of the older shoots
can be eaten in the same way but are not as good.

In the early summer the spikes at the top of the seed
head form clusters of yellow colored pollen which is
very light and fine. It can be stripped from the stalks
with the fingers and put in tight containers or bags to
be used as flour for bread. It is especially good when
mixed with coarser grain flour.

Before the pollen appears, the green head is boiled
and eaten like corn on the cob. When dry, the heads are
burned, leaving only the tiny roasted seeds, which can
be eaten as mush or ground for flour. A large quantity
of cattail heads yields only a small quantity of seeds.

The down, stuffed between two blankets that have

been sewn together, will give excellent insulation in cold weather; stuffed into shoes, it will help prevent frostbite.

The leaves, stripped and dried, can be used to make matting and other woven materials like sandals, baskets, blankets, and ponchos.

## Chicory; *Cichorium intybus*

Description: Chicory leaves resemble the leaves of a dandelion, but the chicory stem is branching and stiff. In late summer, blue flowers appear on the stiff irregular stalks.

Preparation and Uses: The leaves are used for a potherb much the same as dandelions, and the roots are edible in emergencies.

## †Chokecherry; *Prunus virginiana*

Description: Chokecherry, a tree or shrub, is easily recognized in the fall by its clusters of red-black cherries. The bark is reddish grey and somewhat speckled with lateral lines that resemble those on the bark of the domestic cherry tree. (See p. 222.)

Preparation and Uses: The cherries of this tree are an excellent food despite the cyanogenetic poison contained in the seed. Slightly dried and crushed—seeds and all— on a mortar and dried in cakes, these berries provide nourishment that is lasting and satisfying. Before they are eaten, the dried cakes must be cooked to help drive off the poison from the seeds. Pemmican is made by mixing fat and pounded dried meat with the meal of chokecherries and sealing it in gut or molding it into round balls for preservation.

## Cottonwood; *Populus*

Description: Large trees growing along streams at most elevations, the cottonwoods have rough grey bark and bear flowers in drooping catkins that are borne in broad disks. The buds of these trees are resinous, and the leaves are serrate with long petioles. (See p. 222.)

Preparation and Uses: The buds and leaves often provide a honeydew made by aphids that is edible. It is scraped from the leaves or skimmed off the surface of the water in which the leaves have been boiled. The inner bark and the sap of the tree are also useful emergency foods.

## Currant; *Ribes*

Description: A shrub three to ten feet tall, the currant has toothed leaves and berries forming in clusters. The berries are gold, red, or black. (See p. 223.)

Preparation and Uses: The berries ripen early and provide excellent food which can be eaten fresh or dried. They may be prepared in any of the ways mentioned for chokecherries. None are known to contain poisonous principles, and they can be used in large amounts.

## †Elderberry; *Sambucus*

Description: Elderberry, a large shrub, is characterized by a large, pithy, brown colored stem bearing opposite compound leaves. The berries grow in flat-topped clusters and are deep purple or red when ripe. (See pp. 223-24.)

Preparation and Uses: The ripe berries in the fall are an important food and can be eaten raw or cooked.

They keep well when dried and often lose their rank flavor. The flower clusters may be eaten dipped in a batter and fried or crushed into stew. The green leaves and stems of the plant are said to be poisonous. The pith of this plant is poisonous.

## Evening Primrose; Oenothera

Description: Evening primrose is either a low growing plant with large white flowers or a somewhat taller plant with yellow flowers. The low growing species is coarse with long leaves growing from the crown of the root. The taller species is rather stiff and erect and may appear to be prickly and coarse. The flowers of all the plants remain open during the night. (See p. 224.)

Preparation and Uses: The seeds of various species can be eaten parched or ground into meal. Many of the species have bitter roots that are not very palatable, but some lose this property when dug in early spring and cooked. When made palatable, the roots are an important source of food in foothills and mountains.

## Goldenrod; Solidago

Description: Goldenrod is a tall plant with a long inflorescence crowded in a cluster and leaves that are often toothed, hairy, and alternate on the stem. (See p. 224.)

Preparation and Uses: The seeds are gathered for food and used for mush and thickening for stew. The young leaves and flowers make a potherb and tea.

## Ground Cherry, Husk Tomato; Physalis

Description: A low trailing plant, ground cherry bears yellow flowers that later form into balloonlike husks or bladders. Inside each bladder is a small fruit which resembles a tomato. The leaves of the plant are usually oblong or ovate and bluntly pointed. (See p. 225.)

Preparation and Uses: The fruit makes a good ingredient for stew and may also be eaten raw. It can even be baked in dough for small pies.

## Groundsel; *Senecio*

Description: Groundsel is usually found in moist or wet meadows. The leaves are mostly basal, lance shaped, and dissected into narrow divisions, and its flowers are yellow. The entire plant is covered with tiny hairs that impart a grey color sheen, and its seeds have silky white hairs at the top. The plant also contains a sticky sap. (See p. 225.)

Preparation and Uses: The young leaves are edible as a potherb. They are also often used to line cooking pits and then eaten with other foods prepared in the same pit.

## Hairgrass; *Deschampsia*

Description: Hairgrass is a fine grass of higher altitudes bearing narrow, firm leaf blades and spikelets which are sometimes purple and white. It is found in wet or damp soils. (See p. 225.)

Preparation and Uses: The seeds may be harvested with a seed beater and ground for mush and flour.

## Heron's Bill, Storkbill; *Erodium cicutarium*

Description: An herb which may form rosettes and later have spreading stems, heron's bill bears rose to lavender flowers. The stalks are covered with short hairs, and the seed pod resembles the stork's bill. These plants grow in open dry ground throughout the West. (See p. 226.)

Preparation and Uses: The young plants are cooked for greens or eaten raw as salad.

## Horsetail, Scouring Rush, Joint Grass, Snake Grass; *Equisetum*

Description: Horsetail is the common joint grass so eagerly sought after by children for playthings. The stems are of two kinds: one is sterile and has many branches; the other is fertile and has no branches. The grass is jointed and pulls apart easily, and at the top of the fertile plant is a brown head. (See p. 226.)

Preparation and Uses: The young shoots in the spring can be used as a potherb during emergencies. Later the shoots become too stiff and contain a silica that gives them the name "scouring rush." They can then be used for cleaning metal, for polishing and honing bone implements and wooden shafts, and for sharpening pocketknives.

## Indian Potato; *Orogenia linearifolia*

Description: Indian potato is a tiny plant with basal leaves that are divided into slender leaflets that look like bird tracks. The stem arises from a deep nutlike bulb, and the tiny white flowers grow in compound umbels. (See p. 227.)

Preparation and Uses: This was a favorite of the Indians, who used it frequently for food. The bulb can be boiled, steamed, roasted, or baked in any of the ways used for preparing potatoes. However, the tiny bulbs are also tasty when eaten raw. They may be cooked and mashed into cakes for drying; they keep indefinitely when protected from moisture. The hard cakes can then be soaked and cooked in stew or soup. One of the tastiest roots found in the West, this plant grows in meadows and on mountainsides at higher altitudes.

## Indian Ricegrass; *Oryzopsis hymenoides*

Description: Indian ricegrass has slender stems and flat or in-rolled leaves and a tufted seed head which contains large grains. This plant is found on sand dunes and desert areas. (See p. 227.)

Preparation and Uses: The seeds are ground for cereal. This grain is abundant and easily harvested.

## Jerusalem Artichoke, Sunflower; *Helianthus tuberosus*

Description: A species of sunflower introduced from the Midwest and found growing in waste areas, jerusalem artichoke is usually more slender than the native sunflower of the West. It has large potatolike roots in the fall. (See p. 228.)

Preparation and Uses: The large tuber is edible and formed an important food for the Indians of the Midwest. It has largely escaped cultivation in the West and is not generally found in unsettled areas.

## Juniper, Cedar; *Juniperus*

Description: Evergreen shrubs or trees with blue berries, junipers are very common in the foothills and desert portions of the West. (See pp. 228-29.)

Preparation and Uses: The blue berries of the junipers are bitter but nutritious and can be eaten in an emergency. If they are pounded and boiled, some of the bitter, resinous taste is removed. The inner white bark, stripped and pounded into a meal, will hold off starvation for a time.

## Lamb's Quarter, Goosefoot; *Chenopodium*

Description: Lamb's quarter is a common weed of wastelands and stream banks. The leaves vary from ovate to lanceolate in the various species, and its seeds form in clusters. (See p. 229.)

Preparation and Uses: The leaves and stems are edible when young. They can be eaten as salad or cooked like spinach. The seeds are also edible; they are ground into flour and used for making bread.

## Mallow, Cheese Weed; *Malva*

Description: Annual plants with thick roots and stems that run along the ground, mallows bear small white to pale blue flowers. The fruit is round and flattened into the shape of a cheese wheel, hence the name *cheesies*. These plants are found around cultivated areas. (See p. 229.)

Preparation and Uses: Mallows can be used as a potherb, and the leaves and stems may be cooked in soups. The fruit is excellent eaten raw or cooked, and the dried leaves make a superior warm drink.

## Mannagrass; *Glyceria*

Description: Mannagrass has long narrow leaves and a long seed head. It is often found growing on stream banks and around seeps, and its long leaves sometimes hang into the water and float.

Preparation and Uses: The seeds are gathered with a seed beater, winnowed to remove the chaff, and used as a thickening for stews and soups. They can be ground on a metate for flour. Mannagrass is one of the better tasting grains that are found growing in the West.

## Maple, Box Elder; *Acer negundo*

Description: A tree with leaves composed of three to five separate leaflets and winged seeds, the box elder is common to mountain valleys and gullies. (See p. 230.)

Preparation and Uses: The winged seeds are roasted and eaten. Pounded for flour, the inner bark serves as an emergency food. When the sap rises in late winter, the sweet sap can be boiled down into a good maple syrup.

## †Milkweed; *Asclepias syriaca*

Description: The stout stems of milkweed bear opposite entire leaves with broad midribs, and when broken, the stems and leaves emit a milky sap. The large pods, formed after flowering, bear seeds that are plumed with silky fibers. (See p. 230.)

Preparation and Uses: Some milkweeds are highly poisonous. However, if the survivalist carefully distinguishes *Asclepias syriaca* milkweed from the deadly dogbane, which is a similar plant, the young shoots of the former can be cooked and eaten. The very young seed pods can be boiled and eaten also. The sap may be heated for chewing gum and the fibers of the stalk used to make cordage and fish line.

## Miner's Lettuce, Indian Lettuce; *Montia*

Description: Indian lettuce is a small succulent plant with round, fleshy leaves. Some of the leaves are joined to each other on both sides in such a way as to form a rounded disk or cup. (See p. 230.)

Preparation and Uses: This tasty plant is the rival of garden lettuce for salads and raw greens and can be eaten in large quantities. When mixed with watercress and placed between two hotcakes made of Indian potato root dough, it is unexcelled for flavor and constitutes a rare and satisfying sandwich.

## Mint; Mentha and other genera

Description: Members of the mint family are characterized by a square stem and opposite leaves. (See p. 231.)

Preparation and Uses: Catnip, peppermint, horehound, spearmint, horsemint, sage, thyme, hyssop, and several other plants of the mint family are used for food and drink. As drinks, some are unmatched for their soothing qualities and often relieve headache, nausea, colic, and other nervous upsets that the survivalist may encounter in the wilds. The seeds can also be eaten or added to the leaves for steeping.

## Mormon Tea, Brigham Tea, Squaw Tea; Ephedra

Description: A shrub with stiff, green colored, jointed branches and scale-like leaves, Mormon tea is found in the southern portions of the West and is easily identified. (See p. 232.)

Preparation and Uses: The green stems can be steeped for a soothing drink, but the beverage may stain the teeth if used regularly.

## Mountain Dandelion, False Dandelion; Agoseris

Description: Mountain dandelion looks like the common dandelion with its yellow flower; however, its leaves may or may not be toothed. (See p. 232.)

Preparation and Uses: The leaves and roots are edible when cooked. The hardened sap or juice from the root and stems is also edible and can be used as chewing gum.

## Mule's Ears; Wyethia

Description: *Wyethia amplexicaulis* has flower heads which resemble those of the sunflower. They are bright or orange yellow, and several heads grow on a stalk. The plant itself grows low to the ground, and its leaves are erect and glossy. *Wyethia helianthoides* is similar in appearance, having white flowers and a sticky, hairy stalk. These two species of mule's ears often cross-produce hybrids which bear yellow flowers on their hairy stalks. (See p. 232.)

Preparation and Uses: The seeds are edible, and the roots of *Wyethia helianthoides* can be eaten after they are cooked for at least thirty hours in a steaming pit.

## Mustard, Shepherds Purse, White top, Peppergrass; Sisymbrium, Brassica, Lepidium, and other genera

Description: These common mustards of every barnyard and of wasteland are evident in several forms. They are generally a leafy weed, erect with yellow or white flowers. The leaves are often deeply cleft. (See pp. 233-34.)

Preparation and Uses: The seeds of all the species are edible, as well as the young greens which are eaten as a potherb.

## Nettle, Stinging Nettle; Urtica

Description: Nettle is an erect plant with opposite toothed leaves that are long and pointed at the outer end. The stalks, stems, and leaves are covered with fine stinging hairs that are well known to most picnickers. (See p. 234.)

Preparation and Uses: The leaves and young stems are edible as cooked greens. They are gathered with gloves or with large mullein leaves (*Verbascum*) used as pads for the hands. The stinging properties leave when the plant is cooked.

### †Oak; *Quercus*

Description: Oak ranges all the way from a shrub six inches high to the small common scrub oak which grows in the mountains to the large tree which grows in fertile valleys. *Q. gambelli* is the most important. (See p. 234.)

Preparation and Uses: The acorn can serve as an emergency food but must be leached of its tannic acid before it is eaten.

### †Onion, Wild Garlic, Nodding Onion; *Allium*

Description: Resembling the domestic onions, these small wild onions and garlics always have the familiar onion smell when their leaves are bruised. Plants looking like onions but lacking the characteristic smell should be checked closely, as some species such as death camas (*Zigadenus*) are very poisonous. Late in the season one can find this small onion plant by first finding the stalk. The dried flower head on the stalk looks like a white ball against the ground. (See p. 235.)

Preparation and Uses: The whole plant is edible raw or cooked and is an excellent addition to any dish.

### Oregon Grape, Algerita; *Mahonia*

Description: Oregon grape is a shrub with hollylike leaflets which grows low to the ground in dense thickets and under trees. Its leaves are spined and dark green. In the Southwest, other species often form large bushes or even trees bearing palatable fruit. (See pp. 235-36.)

Preparation and Uses: The deep purple or red berries are edible raw or cooked and are rather tasty and tart. They can also be dried for future use.

## Piñon Pine; *Pinus monophylla, P. edulis*

Description: An evergreen tree which grows in many areas of the West, the piñon pine is characterized by its spreading growth and dense covering of pine cones containing large seeds. The cones of most pine trees do not bear these large seeds. (See p. 236.)

Preparation and Uses: The cones are gathered and charred in a fire. In this way the seeds are roasted and loosened. Then they are beaten from the cones and used as one of the most important foods available in nature. They may be eaten shelled or ground up, shell and all, on a metate.

## Plantain; *Plantago major, P. lanceolata*

Description: Plantain, a common lawn pest, grows in two varieties. *Plantago major* has flat leaves and *Plantago lanceolata*, long lance-shaped leaves, both of which are dark green and ribbed. The seed heads grow in dense clusters at the end of long stems. The whole plant is only about eight inches tall. (See p. 236.)

Preparation and Uses: The young leaves can be eaten and are also an important herb for dressing wounds (see Medicinal Plants, p. 108).

## Prickly Lettuce, Wild Lettuce; *Lactuca*

Description: A common weed, prickly lettuce is characterized by several species, most of them having narrow leaves that are lobed. The plant bleeds a milky juice when injured. (See p. 237.)

Preparation and Uses: The young leaves are edible when cooked, and the gum of the roots is made into chewing gum.

## Prickly Pear Cactus; *Opuntia*

Description: The prickly pear cacti have pear-shaped pads and fruits, and large patches grow on hillsides and deserts throughout the West. Many other cacti are edible but should be identified before they are eaten. (See pp. 237-38.)

Preparation and Uses: The fruits and new joints of this plant should be scorched or peeled. They can be eaten raw or cooked, and the seeds can be ground into flour. Some cacti may be over a hundred years old; care should be used so as not to destroy them.

## Purslane; *Portulaca oleracea*

Description: A small weed growing low to the ground, purslane has smooth, fleshy leaves with rounded ends and stems that are usually rose colored and juicy. (See p. 238.)

Preparation and Uses: The whole plant is edible as a salad green or as a potherb.

## †Rabbitbrush; *Chrysothamnus*

Description: Rabbitbrush, a stiff light colored brush with new green stems at the top, grows in alkaline soils, usually around water holes and lakes. (See p. 238.)

Preparation and Uses: The survivalist must be aware that rabbitbrush is poisonous to livestock. However, the new tips of the brush are edible in the spring and the secretion at the top of the roots can be chewed for gum.

## Raspberry, Thimbleberry, Black Cap; *Rubus*

Description: All species are shrubs, some having spines with red, black, purple, blue, or orange berries, and all belong to the rose family. The common wild raspberry is perhaps the most prevalent. (See p. 239.)

Preparation and Uses: The berries are edible in season and can be dried for future use.

## Red Clover; *Trifolium*

Description: These wild red clovers resemble the domestic variety with its round flower head and three leaves. (See p. 239.)

Preparation and Uses: The seeds are edible as well as the greens, and the steeped leaves and flowers are reputed to be good for colds and coughs.

## Reed, Reed Canary Grass; *Phragmites communis*

Description: Long jointed and stout with hollow stems, reed resembles cane or bamboo. (See p. 239.)

Preparation and Uses: The seeds are edible when cooked as cereal. The roots may also be eaten when cooked, and the young shoots eaten raw or cooked. The plant's main value is its use in weaving and in the manufacturing of arrowshafts.

## Rose, Wild Rose; Rosa

Description: Every camper knows this thorny bush. This rose is similar to the domestic rose bush and usually has reddish colored stems bearing bright red fruit that matures in the fall after the first frost. (See p. 240.)

Preparation and Uses: The rose hips or berries are a ready supply of nutritious food that lasts through the fall and often all winter. They are easily picked and ground on a metate for a meal or for flour, but the fresh fruit is also good when cooked. The numerous seeds are hard and must be cracked or ground before they are eaten. Rose hips contain a massive dose of vitamin C and are very nourishing.

## Salsify, Oysterplant, Goatsbeard; Tragopogon

Description: The leaves of salsify are grasslike and slightly hairy, giving them a queer translucent appearance around the edges. The second-year plants produce yellow or purple flowers that later form large seed heads with umbrellalike fluffs that carry the seeds away in the wind. (See pp. 240-41.)

Preparation and Uses: The first-year roots are edible when cooked, but as the first-year plant produces only leaves without flowers, it is often hard to recognize. The root of the second-year plant tastes like steamed oysters and is a rich wilderness food.

## Samphire; *Salicornia*

Description: Small, light green, and branching, samphire has fleshy stems reaching up like claws and is found in saline bogs and marshes. (See p. 241.)

Preparation and Uses: The plant is edible raw or cooked and is a rich source of salt. Added to stew, it provides all the salt flavoring necessary.

## Sego Lily; *Calochortus*

Description: The small grasslike leaves of the sego lily grow among brush and trees in the foothills. Later a stem appears bearing a lovely yellow, creamy white, or bluish flower with light purple splotches at the base of the petals. As it is the state flower of Utah, it should be harvested only in emergencies or for scientific purposes. At one time the plant was thought to be almost extinct; it now grows abundantly in many areas although much less widespread than formerly. Some of the plants do not bloom, which often leads the layman to believe that this species is rare. (See p. 241.)

Preparation and Uses: The tender bulb, harvested with a digging stick, is unsurpassed in flavor when roasted or boiled and can also be cooked and mashed into cakes for preservation.

## Service Berry; *Amelanchier*

Description: The service berries, shrubs or small trees, have simple leaves and blue colored fruit that resembles tiny apples when ripe. (See p. 242.)

Preparation and Uses: The berries may be cooked or dried, mashed into cakes for drying, or mixed with dried meat for pemmican.

## †Sour Dock, Sorrel, Curly Dock, Yellow Dock, Wild Rhubarb, Indian Tobacco; *Rumex*

Description: The stems of sour dock are grooved, resembling rhubarb, and the flowers grow in clusters and form large seed clusters that turn brown in the fall. (See p. 242.)

Preparation and Uses: If chopped and then boiled for a long time into syrup, the stems are especially good. If not too bitter, they may be eaten raw like rhubarb, but the leaves may be toxic if they contain too much oxalic acid.

## Spring Beauty; *Claytonia lanceolata*

Description: A tiny plant, spring beauty is found in wooded areas and grows from a round nutlike corm. Its small white or pink flowers bloom early in the spring, and its leaves grow opposite on the stem in one pair. (See p. 243.)

Preparation and Uses: An important source of food in the spring, the small bulbs are dug with a digging stick and can be prepared in any of the ways used to prepare potatoes. They also preserve readily after they are cooked and mashed into cakes for drying.

## Strawberry, Wild Strawberry; *Fragaria americana*

Description: This strawberry is like the domestic variety, only smaller. (See p. 243.)

Preparation and Uses: The berry is eaten in season and the leaves are steeped for an excellent hot drink.

## Sumac, Squawbush; *Rhus trilobata*

Description: Sumac is a sprawling shrub with a three-lobed leaf or with three leaflets to a leaf that has broad outer ends; its berries form in clusters and are very sticky. (See p. 243.)

Preparation and Uses: The berries serve as an emergency food and an even better drink. Steeped in water and drunk cold, they are very refreshing.

## Sunflower; *Helianthus*

Description: This is the common sunflower easily recognized by almost anyone. It has flowers in a large yellow head and rather prickly, hairy stalks. (See p. 244.)

Preparation and Uses: The seeds of sunflowers are perhaps the most nourishing food found in the wilds. Harvested with a seed beater and then ground on a metate, they are used as mush. They should not be cooked, but just heated or eaten cold. They also make an excellent baby food; the Indians depended on them to a great extent for that purpose.

## Thistle; *Cirsium*

Description: Many species of thistle exist, but generally they all may be described as succulent plants with many spines on the leaves and stems. (See p. 244.)

Preparation and Uses: The young tender plant stems can be peeled and eaten, and the roots are good when boiled with other food.

## Thornapple, Haw, Hawthorn; *Crataegus*

Description: Thornapple is the only native tree with thorns of any size. It looks somewhat like an apple tree, its fruit resembling miniature apples.

Preparation and Uses: The berries are good food when dried and made into cakes. The dried cakes, ground and mixed with pounded jerky, make pemmican.

## Umbrella Plant, Trumpet Plant, Wild Buckwheat; *Eriogonum*

Description: The leafless stalks of the umbrella plant are topped by compound umbels of tiny yellow or cream colored flowers, and the stem arises from a dense cluster of leaves which are matted on the ground. The leaves are usually lance shaped and are white on the bottom side. The plant grows in open areas of dry soil up to 9,000 feet. (See p. 244.)

Preparation and Uses: The leaves are cooked for greens, and the seeds are edible after they are ground on a metate into meal or into flour for making bread.

## Violet, Dogtooth, Glacier Lily; *Erythronium grandiflorum*

Description: In spite of its name, violet is not a violet but a lily with a yellow flower and two large shiny oblong leaves arising from the base. The petals are very recurved, and the bulb is deep and rounded. The plant grows at higher altitudes along streams and in shaded woodlands. (See p. 245.)

Preparation and Uses: The bulb is dug with a digging stick but is difficult to obtain because it grows so deep. The bulbs are excellent when cooked like potatoes, and they can also be cooked and mashed for storage. In addition, the leaves are edible as greens. The violet is a rare plant and should be used only in emergencies.

## Watercress; *Nasturtium officinale*

Description: Green and leafy and growing in clear water, watercress has white threadlike roots that form thick mats along the edges of streams. The leaves of this plant have three to nine segments. Watercress also bears tiny white flowers. (See p. 245.)

Preparation and Uses: Watercress, which has a pleasant tangy taste, is a favorite salad plant used raw as greens. Watercress and miner's lettuce or *Montia*, when they are wrapped together in tortillas made from root flour, make the survivalist an excellent wilderness sandwich.

## Waterleaf; *Hydrophyllum*

Description: The delicate waterleaf grows at higher altitudes on damp hillsides among dense growth of brush and trees. Its flower is a globular head of tiny white or purple flowers, and its leaves are broad, fleshy, and deeply divided, with rounded tips. (See p. 245.)

Preparation and Uses: The whole plant is edible. The rootstalks, which are several tiny brown carrotlike appendages radiating from the base of the stem, make excellent stew and the plant tops serve as greens.

## Wheat Grass, Blue Joint Grass, Quack Grass; *Agropyron*

Description: This is the common wheat grass and other similar species that are found throughout the West. It has a wheatlike seed head that contains a nutritious grain.

Preparation and Uses: The seeds are harvested with a seed beater and ground on a metate. They can be gathered in goodly amounts with a little patience. The rootstalks of this plant are also edible.

### †Wild Hyacinth; *Brodiaea*

Description: Wild hyacinth has slender basal leaves and flowers—usually blue—that grow in clusters forming umbels. It is easily confused with camas or wild onions when not in bloom. Also the name *hyacinth* is misleading, for domestic hyacinth is poisonous. (See p. 246.)

Preparation and Uses: The bulb, an important food source in higher elevations, is best cooked and eaten with greens or mashed and dried for future use in stews. Harvesting it with a digging stick is difficult because it grows deep.

### Wild Rye; *Elymus*

Description: A common bunch grass seen along roadsides and in deserts, wild rye is tall and coarse. The plants are characterized by their flat leaves, and they bear a single erect spike of seeds at the end of each stem.

Preparation and Uses: The seeds are harvested by stripping or with a seed beater. Carefully winnowed, they make an excellent grain for mush and flour if the chaff is singed.

### †Yampa, Wild Caraway; *Perideridia*

Description: A slender plant, yampa grows on damp hillsides and meadows in the foothills of the plateau area. The leaves are compound with narrow grasslike leaflets and usually dry up by flowering time. The flowers are borne in small white compound umbels. This plant is a member of the carrot family and positive identification is necessary before it is eaten. Typically, fruit is required for positive identification.

Preparation and Uses: The small fingerlike roots grow deep and sometimes form in groups of two or three. Perhaps some of the most important and tastiest roots found, they far outrank potatoes in flavor, and can be cooked in any of the ways used for potatoes. When cooked and mashed into cakes for drying, they keep indefinitely.

### Yellow Fritillary, Yellowbell; *Fritillaria pudica*

Description: The small yellow fritillary has lanceolate, basal leaves and a single yellow or golden flower that hangs either sideways or down from the bent stalk. The root is a corm with a cluster of tiny rice-like bulblets surrounding it. The plant grows among the brush on damp hillsides. (See p. 246.)

Preparation and Uses: The corm is edible, as are the rice-like bulblets and when cooked, they resemble rice in both appearance and taste. The green seed heads can also be eaten after they are cooked.

## Medicinal Plants

Plants are necessary to the survivalist not only as food but also as mild medicine. The following plants have been tested in the field for their medicinal value and have proved most helpful to people who have suffered from minor irritations, wounds, and burns while in the wilds.

## Biscuit-root, Kouse; *Cymopterus*

The old roots of biscuit-root are an effective insecticide when boiled. (See p. 217.)

## Burdock; *Arctium minus*

The young roots of the first-year burdock dug in early spring or late fall are often used as a salve or wash for burns, wounds, and skin irritations. (See pp. 219-20.)

## Cattail; *Typha*

The white starchy roots of the cattail are pounded and mixed with animal fat and used as a salve in dressing burns. (See p. 221.)

## Chokecherry; *Prunus virginiana*

The inner bark of chokecherry is sometimes used as a tea to check diarrhea. (See p. 222.)

## Mullein; *Verbascum thapsus*

The burned leaves of mullein, used as an incense, are useful in relieving lung congestion. (See p. 233.)

## Nettle, Stinging Nettle; *Urtica*

The root and leaves of nettle, when drunk as a tea, are good for stopping diarrhea, but can cause constipation. (See p. 234.)

## Onion, Wild Garlic, Nodding Onion; *Allium*

The smashed leaves of wild onions, rubbed on the arms and neck, are an effective insect repellent. However, the leaves, because of their offensive odor, are also a very effective people repellent. (See p. 235.)

## Peppermint; *Mentha piperita*

Peppermint is an aromatic stimulant and will often relieve nausea, colic, nervous headache, and heartburn.

## Pines; *Pinus*

The pitch of the lodgepole pine is useful for disinfecting and protecting open sores. The young shoots of the western white pine are boiled and used as cough syrup or as a mild drink for treating coughs and upset stomachs.

## Plantain; *Plantago*

The fresh leaves of plantain act as a mild astringent when mashed to a pulp and applied to cuts and other wounds. They are also highly recommended for quick relief of the external rectal irritation of piles. (See p. 236.)

## Rose, Wild Rose; *Rosa*

Very rich in vitamins A and C, wild rose "hips" are used as a tea or eaten raw. (See p. 240.)

### Service Berry; *Amelanchier*

The boiled green inner bark of service berry is used for an eyewash. (See p. 242.)

### Sour Dock; *Rumex crispus*

The roots of curly dock are mashed and used for a poultice on sores and swellings. (See p. 242.)

### Sweet Flag; *Acorus calamus*

The root of sweet flag, when steeped and drunk as a tea, relieves upset stomach.

### Yarrow; *Achillea millefolium*

The leaves of yarrow are used to stop bleeding in wounds, to reduce inflammation, and to heal rashes when applied directly to the wounded area. They can also be used for tea and can relieve toothache when chewed. (See p. 246.)

### Directions for Gathering Botanicals

- Leaves of biennials are most valuable during their second year of growth. Leaves should always be collected in clear dry weather in the morning after the dew is off and are at their best when the plant is in bloom.
- Flowers are worth more medicinally if used as soon as they open.
- Bulbs and roots are more useful if gathered at the time the leaves of the plant die in the autumn.
- Only the inner bark, preferably gathered in the fall, should be used.

**6**

Fig. 58. Hunting and killing—justified only by sincere need

# ANIMALS

Animal life is an important and substantial source of food for the survivalist. But the hunting and trapping of animals for that purpose and for other needs, such as clothing and tools, requires a great deal of prowess and patience. One must be trained in order to be a good hunter and trapper, and he must observe a certain code of conduct during that training. All life, from a tiny insect to a hot-tempered moose, has a sacred right to fulfill the measure of its creation and in no way does this fulfillment require that a beast become sport for man. Hunting for existence is a different proposition altogether and reflects a more serious and mature relationship with nature. Hunger is humbling and killing creates a void in the earth that is justified not by a shelf laden with trophies but rather by sincere need (Fig. 58).

Hunting an animal is a challenge, and if a need for the animal is present, one can certainly enjoy that challenge. However, need implies putting the animal to good use; in other words every part of it should be used for survival. To waste even a shred is inexcusable.

The methods used to obtain game in a primitive situation are varied, but many are cruel and should be avoided unless no other means presents itself.

Every resource for gathering in meat must be considered and used. If one puts all of his effort into hunting larger game, he usually ends up with only an empty stomach. Therefore, trapping small game and harvesting insects are a must in most areas. Hunting, then, should be second nature to the survivalist, but it should not receive the main emphasis.

## Insects

Some insects provide a life-saving source of food in an emergency and can often be found in profusion after a hatch. If properly harvested, they can insure a food supply for several days. On the other hand, the survivalist may have to be content with an occasional grub to add to his stew. When he forages, he should never disregard the lone grasshopper because he thinks it is too insignificant to matter. The nutritional value of insects is high and adds substantially to a meager diet. However, *all insects must be cooked,* as they harbor internal parasites that are very harmful to human beings.

One must be careful not to expend more energy harvesting food than that which the food can replace. In particular, catching insects such as grasshoppers can become exasperating and tiring unless one learns a few tricks.

Listed here are some of the more common insects which provide good food. Also listed are appropriate methods of harvesting them and uses to which they can be put.

## Grasshoppers, Locusts, Crickets, and Katydids, *Orthoptera*

Uses: If there are enough of these insects, they can be roasted and dried, ground into meal, and served in soups and stews. Small amounts can be boiled or roasted and served whole in soups or stews.

Harvesting Methods: At night grasshoppers climb tall plants and cling to the stalks near the top and can be picked from the plants early in the morning while they are chilled and dormant. When grasshoppers are located in large quantities, several people can drive them with switches to one side of a meadow or clearing. The grasshoppers can then be caught as they are swatted with willow switches. They can be roasted and eaten on the spot, however. One does this by driving the grasshoppers into rows of dry grass previously prepared for catching them and setting the grass on fire. Grasshoppers and locusts in large amounts are available in some locales from late July until late August, usually in mountain meadows and plateau regions of the West.

## Stone flies and other nymphs, *Plecoptera*

Uses: Nymphs can be boiled in soups and stews with other food.

Harvesting Methods: Nymphs inhabit the undersides of stones in fast-moving streams and crawl on the water's edge in the early spring. They are simply picked from the stones and grass stems and stored in a wet container until they are needed for cooking.

## Cicadas, *Homoptera*

Uses: The wings of the adult cicada are plucked, and then the insect is boiled in stew.

Harvesting Methods: Cicadas are found in juniper trees and brush in desert regions and can be harvested in the early morning in the same manner as that used for grasshoppers. Cicadas can be located when they make a loud clicking noise somewhat similar to the sound of rattlesnakes.

## Ants, *Hymenoptera*

Uses: Ants in quantity may be roasted, ground into powder, and used as an addition to soups and stews. When the ants are roasted, the abdomen usually separates from the rest of the body and can be winnowed to produce a sweet black sugar.

Harvesting Methods: Carpenter ants are found in dead trees and stumps and may be gathered by hand as they are quite large. Smaller red and black ants build rather large mounds around areas of vegetation, constructing them from small sticks and other vegetable matter. One method of harvesting ants calls for planting a deep container in the midst of a mound having the top level of the container level with the surface of the mound. When the den is stirred up, the ants fall into the container. A more elaborate method, used by desert Indians, calls for the ants to be parched. A whole den of them is first shoveled onto a winnowing tray made of willow shoots. Next, the whole trayful is covered with a layer of hot coals. Then it is picked up, and the entire mass is winnowed. The hot coals kill and roast the ants as they are gradually winnowed from the coals. During this process the chaff is also winnowed from the mound.

## Grubs and Caterpillars

Uses: There are many varieties of grubs and caterpillars that can be utilized in soups and stews, but those with hair or fuzz on them should be avoided as some are poisonous.

Harvesting Methods: Grubs are usually located in rotten logs and stumps, but are seldom found in quantity. Caterpillars usually infest a small area and can provide protein for several meals.

# Reptiles and Amphibians

The best tool for snake hunting is a digging stick (Fig. 47, p. 67). Making a special snake stick is a waste of time in a survival situation and just adds to the bulk of the gear. It is imperative that no one play with or tease a rattlesnake before killing it. After the snake is dead its head should be cut off and buried. This is especially necessary if anyone in the group has bare feet.

All reptiles and amphibians should be skinned and eviscerated before they are cooked. Snakes and lizards are the most common reptiles, but at best provide only meager sustenance for the amount of effort required to prepare them (Fig. 59). Frogs are a good source, however, when they are found in quantity in marsh areas.

It is a simple matter to shoot frogs with three-pronged arrows and a crude bow. The arrows should be long— more like spears than arrows (Fig. 60). Reed grass and cattail spikes make the best shafts, but the foreshafts or prongs should be made from hardwood. For these greasewood (*Sarcobatus*) is the finest. The bow does not need to be fancy, nor even very strong for such purposes. The distance for shooting frogs is rarely over

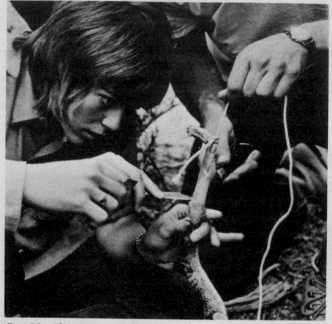

**Fig. 59. Skinning a rattlesnake**

three feet from the tip of the long arrow. The bow merely provides a speedier and more accurate propulsion than can be achieved by thrusting a spear with the arm. Therefore, a green willow bow, cut and made on the spot, will do the job (Fig. 61).

## Birds

Small birds should be considered as emergency food only, for efforts to obtain them are out of proportion to the amount of nourishment they provide.

Larger birds are worthy of one's closer attention, however, and in some areas can provide substantial

Fig. 60. Bow and arrow used for frogs

Fig. 61. Hunting with a bow and arrow

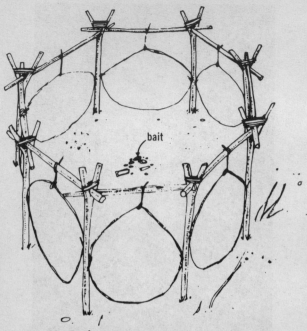

bait

**Fig. 62. Bird snares**

meat for the fire. Chucker partridge, quail, and sage hens are elusive targets even for a shotgun and are difficult to snare and trap. Yet, if the hunter is patient and prepared, he can capture these birds.

One can hunt sage hens successfully with arrows or throwing sticks, and can literally herd chuckers and quail along the ground in narrow canyon areas. These birds will usually not fly unless they are pressed too hard. Snares and nets can be set up in the brush in areas which they frequent, and by making periodic drives, one can literally herd them into his traps (Fig. 62).

With a throwing stick, one of the most effective yet simple weapons for survival, one can obtain more game

Fig. 63. Throwing stick

Fig. 64. Piute deadfall set under a rock

than with any other hunting device. Any hardwood branch will do for a start. However, one should spend time constructing and practicing with a well-made stick that is balanced and beveled to fit the throwing arm (Fig. 63).

Bush and trail snares are also very useful for hunting animals; *however, the hunting of any game animal with traps and snares is forbidden except during an extreme emergency when one is lost in the wilderness.*

Fig. 65. Piute deadfall trigger

trail

Fig. 66. Figure 4 trail deadfall. This is used on game trails where brush is thick and at entrances to burrows and dens. A V-shaped row of stakes fanning away from each approach causes game to go through rather than around the logs.

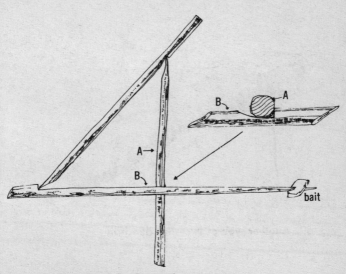

Fig. 67. Details of the figure 4 trap trigger

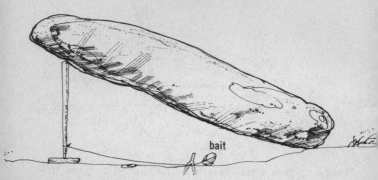

bait

Fig. 68. Two-stick deadfall supporting a flat stone. This is simple to construct, but is not as effective as the figure 4 trap.

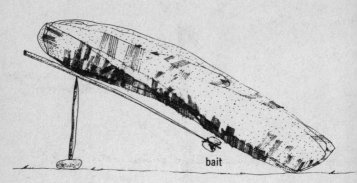

bait

Fig. 69. Another type of two-stick deadfall

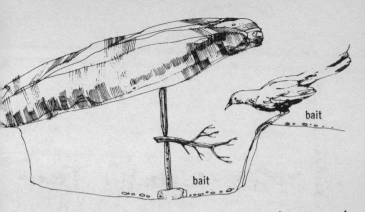

Fig. 70. Bird trap. The bird hops first onto the twig and causes the stone to fall. Rattlesnakes sometimes are caught with this; therefore, one must use caution when retrieving his game.

Fig. 71. Lift pole snare

Fig. 72. Spring pole snare set on a trail. To be caught, the animal must have its front feet in the snare.

Fig. 73. Spring pole snare with baited trigger. The snare loop is placed where it will encircle the animal's neck as it reaches for the bait.

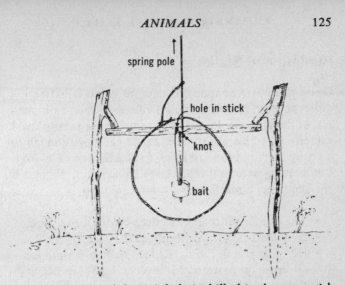

spring pole

hole in stick

knot

bait

Fig. 74. Snare with bait. A hole is drilled in the cross stick and a string threaded through it with a knot in one end, and the bait stick is lightly forced into the hole so that the knot will not slip. A small fence is set up around one side so that the animal must reach through the snare loop to get the bait.

Fig. 75. Trail set snare placed in a feed run made by water animals. The animal drags the stone anchor into the water, sinks, and drowns. A float tied to the stone reveals the position of the snare after it sinks.

## Hunting and Stalking

Using primitive weapons to capture game is extremely different from shooting with a rifle at a deer as it runs across the canyon. In a survival situation a person must exercise all of his ability in order to get close enough to his prey for his arrows or spear to be effective (Fig. 76). But stalking deer and other large game is not difficult if one acquaints himself with a few techniques.

- The hunter must spot the deer before it sees him.
- He must keep downwind from the deer.
- He must watch the deer's feeding habits until he observes a pattern. Most deer feed for about twenty seconds and then raise their heads for a look around. When their heads are down, they see nothing but the brush they are eating.
- The hunter must slowly walk toward the animal when its head is down. As he walks he counts to ten and then stops. He must never press his luck by trying to gain a few more steps before the deer looks up, for it might catch him in the middle of a step. The hunter should make no attempt to hide; instead, he should relax in place, because the wait might be a long one. In a few seconds the deer will raise its head and survey the country but will see only movement. When it looks in the direction of the hunter it might gaze at him for some time, but if the hunter does not even so much as bat an eyelash, the deer will soon ignore him and continue feeding.
- The hunter should walk forward again for another ten seconds as soon as the deer drops its head, and then freeze. The hunter continues this procedure until the range is right for a good shot.

Fig. 76. Hunting with a primitive bow and arrow

Somehow a deer fails to comprehend that what appears to be an old stump gets closer each time the deer looks up.

Deer can also be ambushed at water holes during early dawn hours or in the late evening. The secret here is for one to conceal himself in a spot that does not allow the deer to sense his presence and yet does allow a clear shot. Two or more people can drive deer past hunters concealed along well-used trails.

**Fig. 77. Calling game**

Another technique consists of the hunter calling the animal to him. If he, for instance, learns to mimic the cry of a mouse or rabbit in pain, the hunter will be able to attract any carnivore as well as the animal he imitates. There are a number of ways to make good animal calls but the simplest and perhaps the finest one involves only the lips and the back of the hand. A long, drawn-out kiss on the back of a wet hand sounds (with practice) like a squealing rabbit or mouse. Short smacks sound like the call of a chipmunk or rockchuck. With a little practice a hunter can develop a number of calls using only the lips and hands (Fig. 77).

Rockchucks and ground squirrels may be easily fooled by two hunters who make an open approach to the animal's den, as one of them whistles a lively tune. When the animal dives for his hole, the hunters continue walking and the whistler, still whistling, walks on by and

Fig. 78. Using primitive Indian technique

Fig. 79. Using a rodent skewer

off into the distance. Then the other hunter quickly conceals himself in a position for a good shot and waits. The rockchuck, hearing the whistling fading in the distance, comes out for a look around; and if the concealed hunter is a good shot, he has himself a meal (Fig. 78).

Sometimes a rodent can be dragged from its den with a rodent skewer, a simple device made from a long supple willow with a fork in one end (Fig. 79). The hunter thrusts it into the hole until he feels the animal. Then by gently twisting the stick, he catches the forked end in the animal's fur and winds it tightly. As he gently pulls and coaxes, he brings the rodent to the surface.

Ground squirrels and mice can be caught by flooding them from their holes with a diverted stream or with buckets of water. They can then be killed with sticks as they emerge.

# Fish

Catching fish can be difficult in outdoor survival, but if one learns a few techniques he can end up with enough for a tasty meal.

## Tackle

Making fishing tackle requires some special skills in working bone and in twisting fibers for line. The fibers best suited for this are stinging nettle (*Urtica*), milkweed (*Asclepias*), dogbane (*Apocynum cannabinum*), and the bark of the haw tree (*Crataegus*). They must be selected carefully and twisted tightly (see Cordage, pp. 198-201). Ten feet of line on a long willow pole will serve well in most rivers and streams.

Hooks are best made of bone. The simplest is the

Fig. 80. Skewer hook made from bone

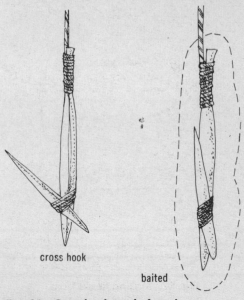

cross hook

baited

Fig. 81. Cross hook made from bone

skewer hook, which is a sliver of bone that is tied at the middle and turned parallel to the line and inserted into the bait (Fig. 80). When the fish swallows the bait, the bone turns sideways and holds. Another simple device is the cross hook, the crosspiece of which is turned parallel to the main shank when the bait is applied. When the fish swallows this, the crosspiece is pulled sideways; thus, the hook is set and the fish is caught (Fig. 81).

Conventional hooks can be made of bone in the following manner:

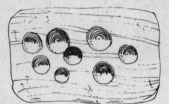

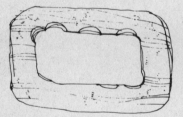

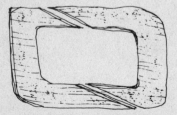

Fig. 82. Making hooks from bird bone

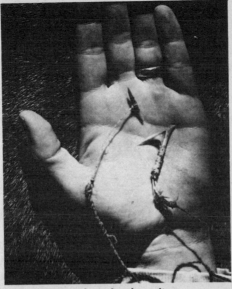

Fig. 83. Attaching hooks to line

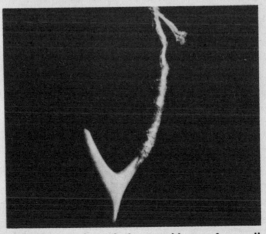

Fig. 84. Hook made from wishbone of a small bird

- A small thin-walled bone (only bird and rodent bones will do) is selected and cut into a rectangle.
- The piece of bone is then drilled several times so that the center portion can be removed.
- The partitions between the drill holes are removed with a stone or bone punch and the walls are smoothed with a small piece of sanding stone. The result is a rectangular ring of bone.
- The ring is then cut in two places, and the result is two hooks which must be sharpened and then attached to a lead line (Fig. 82).

Hooks are attached to the line by a tight wrapping of fine string or fiber. The hook shank is first notched and then smeared with pitch or some other sticky substance. After the wrapping is attached, it is sealed to the hook with pitch. Hooks can be successfully tied on the line without the use of pitch, however, if the wrapping is made tight in the notches (Fig. 83).

Wishbones of small birds may also be used for hooks (Fig. 84).

It is extremely difficult to catch trout and other game fish in small streams with this crude equipment, but river fish such as carp, suckers, catfish, chubs, redhorse, squawfish, and whitefish are easily caught and prove to be very tasty when fried or baked.

## Traps

A good fish trap will catch many more fish than a hook and line. There are several different types, all of which are good. One should build his trap according to the nature of the stream or river—his ingenuity in using natural features to aid in making the traps will determine much of his success (Figs. 85-87).

Fig. 85. Willow fish trap placed in stream riffles between pools

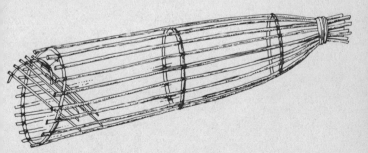

Fig. 86. Willow fish trap. A V-shaped barrier fence made of willows stuck in mud leading to the opening will direct migrating fish into the trap.

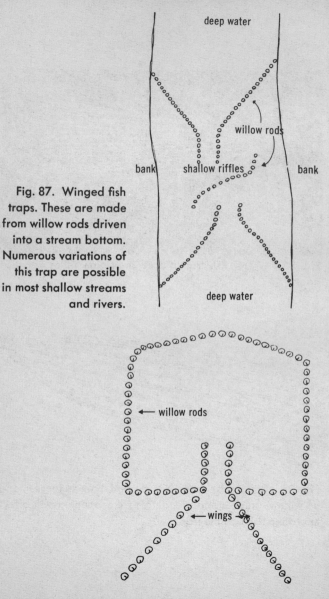

Fig. 87. Winged fish traps. These are made from willow rods driven into a stream bottom. Numerous variations of this trap are possible in most shallow streams and rivers.

## Spears

Many fish feed in shallow water and are easily caught with a simple spear made from a willow about 14 feet long to which is bound a set of hardwood prongs. The prongs should be bound with most of their length attached to the shaft, as this will ensure the sturdiness of the device when it is used roughly. Few fish are lost if one spears them through the sides and then pins them to the bottom by quickly pushing the spear into an upright position and forcing it into the mud (Figs. 88 and 89).

There are also several other types of spears that can be used. However, in a practical sense, none of them will serve any better than the simple one mentioned above. It may prove interesting to try them when the time warrants the effort to manufacture them (Fig. 90).

Fig. 88. Making a fish spear from a willow

Fig. 89. Preparing to spear a fish

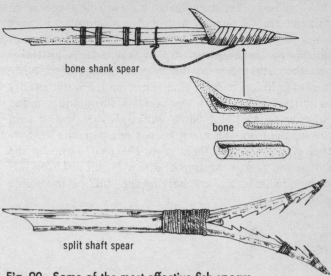

bone shank spear

bone

split shaft spear

**Fig. 90. Some of the most effective fish spears**

## Other Water Life

A good part of the survivalist's food source lives in or near the water, and much of it is so easily caught that a person could live indefinitely from one small stream. Crayfish, mussels, helgramites, stone flies, snails, tiny minnows, and polliwogs are the most common and are found under rocks and moss or in mud along the shore. Crayfish and mussels are the most desirable and can be gathered in fairly large amounts. Mussels are usually found buried in the mud—a shallow trail terminating in a slight hump in the mud will betray their presence. Crayfish appear in the evenings and can be caught by hand or with a hook and line. One can scare them out by moving the rocks which cover them, but they must be grabbed quickly and carefully.

A willow basket trap placed in a swift-flowing stream will net crayfish, small fish, and a multitude of other water life if a proper drive is made. The survivalist can do this by situating the trap so that it faces upstream and then staking it to the bottom or having another person hold it securely. Then, entering the water twenty or thirty feet upstream, he begins kicking and scuffing rocks and gravel and slowly works his way downstream toward the trap. He moves every stone and stirs the bottom vigorously. He then raises the trap, removes the catch, and places the trap in a new location. Using this technique he often catches buckets full of incredible edibles.

## Jerky

Meat will not keep very long in warm weather; therefore, it is necessary that any surplus be dried for future use. The standard modern methods of making jerky involve brines and spices which give the meat a rich flavor. However, these processes decrease the food value and render the meat so salty that a substantial meal of nothing but jerky would make a person sick.

Meat jerked for use as a food rather than as a snack or delicacy must be prepared without brines and spices. It is merely cut into thin strips about ¼ inch thick and dried in the sun for a couple of days. When it becomes hard and brittle, it is taken down and stored in a pit or in bags. It is then used in stews and soups or roasted lightly on the coals and eaten (Fig. 91).

Cutting meat into strips may be difficult when small chunks are involved; therefore, it is easiest if one takes a chunk and cuts through it within ¼ inch of the other side. Then by turning the knife sideways, he can cut or unroll the chunk into a long strip for drying (Fig. 92).

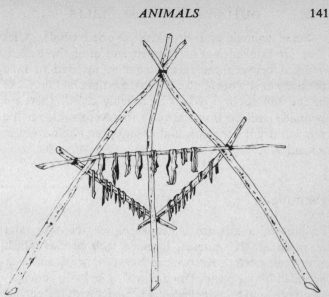

Fig. 91. Jerky hung out to dry

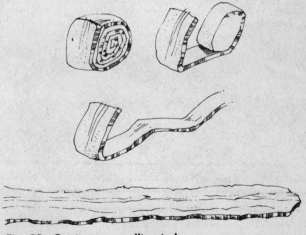

Fig. 92. Cutting or unrolling jerky

Small animals and birds can be dried whole. After they are skinned and eviscerated and after the back is cracked between the legs, a stick is inserted to hold the body cavity open. The animals are then laid on rocks in the sun to dry. When thoroughly dried, they are pounded until the bones are crushed. Another day in the sun will dry the marrow and ensure preservation (Figs. 93 and 94).

## Pemmican

Pemmican, a mixture which surpasses the taste and nutrition of "K" rations, is made with berries which have been dried to remove the excess moisture and then pounded into a paste. Dried pounded jerky is added to this paste, and then melted suet is mixed with the berries

Fig. 93. Ground squirrel spread out to dry in the sun

Fig. 94. Pounding jerky

and meat. The mixture is next rolled into small balls and stored in the cleaned intestines of a large animal. Then the intestine sack is tied shut, sealed with suet, and stored in a cool, dry place. Pemmican prepared in this way will keep for several months (Fig. 95). Balls of pemmican are also safely stored in plastic bags or leather bags that are richly soaked in melted suet.

## Dried Fish

Small minnows are easily dried when spread out in the sun, and it is not necessary that they be cleaned. But larger minnows of over 2½ inches long should be

Fig. 95. Pemmican ready for eating

eviscerated and split for drying. The sun will dry small fish in one or two days after which they can be put in bags for safe keeping or placed in a storage pit for preservation (see p. 75).

Drying larger fish is accomplished in one of two ways. The simplest way is to split the fish down the back and hang it on a rack. Even though the bones are still intact and make eating difficult, one can get around them by pounding the dried fish into a fine meal to be used in stews. This crushes the larger bones, and the finer ones are softened by cooking.

A second method is to fillet the fish and dry the strips by hanging them on a rack in the sun. One cuts the meat from the bones after he splits the fish down the back and removes the side strips by slicing along the ribs. There is some waste if the bones are not saved, however. And in a survival situation waste is not tolerable. The remaining bones can be used well if they are slightly dried and then ground into a meal to be added to stews.

All dried fish will keep a year or more if it is stored in a dry place. Eating dried fish is not always a pleasant experience at first, and there always exists the possibility of parasites. Therefore, it is best to cook the fish before it is eaten.

The advantage to pounding or grinding it is that these processes allow the fish to dry better, thus minimizing spoilage and reducing the space taken up by bulky chunks. The fish meal has many more uses than the whole strips—it can be used in bread, soup, stew, and stuffing; mixed with cooked seed grains for a wholesome cereal; and moistened, made into fish patties, and fried.

**7**

Fig. 96. Straightening an arrow shaft

# SPECIAL SKILLS

In an outdoor survival situation, man can use only the natural elements around him for constructing tools; therefore, he must know how to use nature effectively (Fig. 96). The following explanations of a few of the more important methods of making and using primitive tools will be helpful, but one must realize that common sense is the key and that many other methods will also work.

The skills discussed here are presented exactly as the author has used them while living off the land. They appear in this order: working stone, working bone, constructing bows and arrows, constructing atlatls and spears, making cordage, preparing sinew, weaving sandals and baskets, making rawhide, and tanning skins.

## Working Stone

Ancient man's survival depended in great measure upon his ability to utilize and modify his immediate surroundings. To accomplish the tasks of cutting, digging, scraping, chopping, and building, he developed a remarkable array of tools made of stone. The skills required to produce such workable tools are more complex than one might imagine and show evidence of a high degree of inventiveness and manual dexterity. The amount of work that can be done with these tools is indeed remarkable.

A person thrown into a primitive survival situation would quickly find his existence greatly impaired without the aid of so simple a tool as a pocketknife. It would seem that he could never survive without a knife to cut poles for building shelters, to cut shafts for a spear or

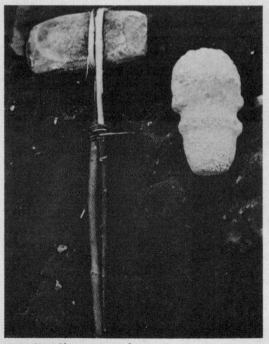

Fig. 97. Chopping tools

Fig. 98. Cutting tools

bow, or to fashion the myriad items essential for survival. The construction of almost everything requires the direct or indirect use of a cutting or chopping tool which is itself fashioned with other tools made with cutting and chopping tools (Figs. 97 and 98).

The more common primitive methods of working stone which are discussed here I carefully researched and repeatedly tested until I achieved mastery of them.

The processes of shaping stone can be divided into four major areas: (1) percussion flaking, (2) pressure flaking, (3) pecking or crumbling, and (4) abrading. Other recognized processes such as incising and piercing are minor and can be included as simple variations of the abrading process under special conditions. They are used exclusively to shape very soft rocks such as soapstone.

## Percussion Flaking

Percussion flaking, a highly technical art demanding precise skill and forethought, consists of three methods: (1) direct percussion with a hammerstone, (2) indirect percussion with a hammerstone and a punch, and (3) direct or indirect percussion with the stone resting on another larger stone (anvil). All three methods can be used in the production of a single piece of work.

Direct percussion, also called direct freehand percussion, can be used for shaping large pieces of rock into blanks from which specialized tools can be fashioned. In practice, the stone to be shaped is held in the left hand and fractured with blows from a hammerstone or horn baton held in the right hand. Simple axes and

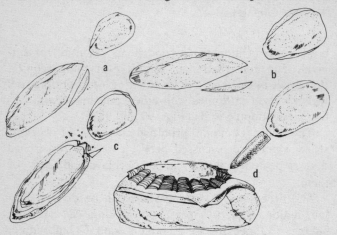

Fig. 99. Striking flakes. (a) Striking directly into hard shale or cobble stone; (b) Striking glassy rock (obsidian or jasper) at an angle with the hammerstone; (c) Striking flakes from glassy stones incorrectly; (d) Striking flakes by indirect percussion.

choppers can be made in this manner from common rhyolite or quartzite cobbles. The blows of the hammerstone should fall directly onto the edge of the core, especially if it is a rather thin one. This is necessary for working chert, coarse agate, dull jasper, or any other nonglassy stone. Holding the blank at an angle while striking off chips is often necessary for removing rough spots and trimming edges. For instance, obsidian and other similar glassy rocks cannot be chipped successfully if they are struck directly on the edge of the core. The core must be struck at an angle if crumbling edges and unwanted hinge fractures are to be avoided (Fig. 99).

When cutting blades or other specialized tools are needed, a striking platform must be constructed on the core. This is done by merely breaking a rock in half, leaving two cores, each with one flat surface. Striking blades from the core is then relatively easy. If the stroke carries all the way through the core, good blades will be produced consistently. If the core is worked around with even strokes, a number of razor-sharp blades can be made before the core is exhausted (Figs. 100 and 101).

If a blank has a difficult knob or thick edge in such a place as to make direct percussion impractical, it can be worked down indirectly with the aid of a punch made from deer horn or other horn of similar density. This process requires the assistance of a second person. The blank is held in the left hand, which is protected with a leather pad, and the punch is placed against the edge of the blank and steadied with the other hand. The assistant then strikes the punch sharply with a hammerstone. In this way the force is applied to the exact spot intended.

Percussion flaking with the blank resting on another stone (anvil) works but is rarely necessary except for

Fig. 100. Striking the core with a horn baton

Fig. 101. Blade struck from the core

removing troublesome knobs and for striking off larger flakes to thin down a thick blank. For this it is best to use the indirect percussion method with the blank resting on a padded anvil.

A variation of the indirect percussion method calls for the blank to be placed between the knees with the edge to be flaked facing up. A person can then use the punch and hammerstone without the aid of an assistant. There is no danger that the chips will cut the knees if the blank is placed in the fold of a thick piece of leather. Variations of this sort are numerous among modern flint-workers and were probably popular in aboriginal times. The use of one method and not another is merely a matter of preference. Basically, the simple use of only the hammerstone or horn baton in shaping tools is the most practical form of percussion flaking.

## Pressure Flaking

The more delicate job of finishing a blank into a specialized implement requires the simplest of tools but a complex nervous system. A nervous Indian probably spent more time bandaging his cuts than making arrowheads. A piece of horn and a leather pad are all that is needed for producing the finest knives and arrowpoints

Fig. 102. Pressure flaking with a horn and a pad

(Fig. 102). A blank or blade produced by percussion flaking or a simple chip of flint or obsidian is held in the palm of the left hand with the fingers gripping it firmly. A leather pad protects the hand from being cut. The hand is braced against the left knee, and small chips are pressed off of the blank with the horn flaker. The tip of the horn is placed on the edge of the flint and pressure is applied inward and downward against it. At the same time, a slight twist is applied to the horn, causing the chip to come off of the underside of the blank. Considerable skill is required for superior work, but one can turn out good serviceable tools in a short time with only a little practice (Fig. 103).

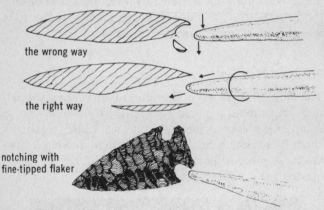

the wrong way

the right way

notching with
fine-tipped flaker

**Fig. 103. Details of pressure flaking**

A further consideration of the minute technicalities of pressure flaking reveals that there is considerably more to it than just the basics previously described.

- The stone must be held slightly forward on the heel of the hand when the stone is gripped in one hand and braced against the knee, so that the pressure from the fingers will tip the edge up.

This allows the flaker tip to force the chip off the bottom side of the blank. Failure to do this can result in quick reduction of the number of fingers on the hand of even the most skilled Stone Age artisan.

- The power of the wrist is not sufficient for flaking larger pieces of stone; hence the force applied with the tip of the flaker must come from the weight of the body. The push should be fairly hard but not sudden. The best results are achieved by just leaning the body into the tip of the flaker with a steady even pressure. Sudden hard lunges cause loss of control and often result in bad cuts.

- The tip of the flaker is not sharpened to a fine point but is given a blunt chisel shape. This allows it to grip the blank firmly.

- The force is applied in the direction in which the flake should run. The objective is to make the flake run across the bottom face of the blank. If the tool is pushed downward at a 90° angle, the flake will be short and stubby.

- The flake comes off more readily if the force of the flaker, as it is applied against the edge of the blank, is accompanied by a slight twist.

The method of pressure flaking described above is the most widely used. One variation of it uses a stone anvil as a rest and is similar to indirect rest percussion. The only difference is that instead of the flakes being struck off they are pressed off with the punch. Here again individual preference is the rule. At any rate, all of the possible methods used for percussion and pressure flaking can be combined and modified to accomplish the task of flaking stone into useful tools.

Horn and leather can also be used for pressure flak-

ing, but only the student trained under civilized exact-
ness would fail to improvise suitable substitutes. The
archaic craftsman caught without his chipping kit would
replace the leather with a pad of sagebrush bark, a flat
piece of tree bark, or some green moss. In place of the
horn, he would use a bone or tooth fragment set in a
wooden handle. He might even use a hardwood stick
or a sliver of rock, though these do not work as well.
The ability to improvise a variety of techniques in working stone cannot be underestimated.

## Pecking or Crumbling

Shaping stones by crumbling them requires relatively
little brainpower, but a lot of perseverance and resigna-
tion to monotony. A caveman working stone probably
often reached the nervous-breakdown point when he
shattered his newly finished axehead with that final per-
fectionist's tap. I can almost hear the canyons ringing
with whatever verbal abuses entered his primeval mind.

The king of stone working implements, the hammerstone, is all that is needed for this process. With it, and
infinite patience, have been shaped colossal stelae and
monumental blocks of solid stone for temples. However,
primitive man, for the most part, was content to use the
simple hammerstone for making axes, clubheads, mor-
tars and pestles, metates and manos, and various other
necessary items (Fig. 104). Hammerstones are best
made from quartzite cobbles and can have a variety of
shapes and sizes. To use them one has only to start
pecking away at another rock, preferably one that is
slightly softer than the hammerstone. The strokes should
be even and rapid, and not too hard, and they should
be kept up until the surface of the stone being shaped
starts to crumble away into a fine dust. The rock being
shaped should never rest on a solid surface as it will

Fig. 104. Using the hammerstone

Fig. 105. Sharpening an axehead

Fig. 106.  Wrapping the handle on

Fig. 107.  Completed hafting of the axehead

crack under the blows of the hammerstone. It should be held loosely in the hand. In this way the tool slowly takes shape. The crumbling process is speeded up if water is applied to the crumbling surface. Axes are generally roughly shaped by percussion flaking with the hammerstone before they are submitted to the crumbling process. A good axehead can be turned out in about one hour, and another hour of grinding and polishing will give it the touch of beauty found in the finest Southwestern stonework (Fig. 105).

One can easily haft an axe by heating a slender willow, wrapping it twice around the axehead, and

Fig. 108. Chopping a willow with the axe

securing it in place by wrapping it with willow shoots or
cord. This type of axe handle will hold tightly and withstand a good deal of abuse (Figs. 106-8). This method
of hafting axes is unequaled for efficiency and ease of
handling.

## Abrading

Grinding, cutting, sawing, drilling, scraping, whetting,
rasping, and polishing are all part of the abrading process. The use of abrasion is important in shaping and
finishing stones used in food preparation, because the
smoothing of grinding implements reduces much of the
grit content in foodstuffs. The cutting edges of implements made of granular stones such as basalt and slate
can be honed to perfection by abrasion.

Grinding and whetting stone simply requires another
stone upon which the implement is rubbed. The best
abrading stones are sandstone and other granular rocks
that contain hard pieces of silica. Sand poured on the
surface of the abrading stone is used as an effective
abrasive. The use of water to speed up the process is
effective. Even the hardest agates can be ground and
polished if they are rubbed against a simple abrasive.
Like the crumbling process, abrasion takes time and
patience. Except for honing cutting edges and smoothing food-grinding implements, grinding and polishing
stone are largely used for giving a finished look to tools
that are already serviceable.

Cutting or sawing stone is accomplished not with a
tooth-edged stone saw but by simple abrasion with thin
slabs of an abrasive stone. Jade and other tough materials are beautifully carved and grooved with simple
slab saws and the use of sand and water as abrasive
agents.

Drilling stone is accomplished in a number of ways,

but the most common method consists of a pump drill with a stone bit. The bit is necessarily made of very hard material, jasper and agate being the finest. With a good pump drill it is a simple matter to drill slate, chert, basalt, rhyolite, or any other soft stone. Even hard stone can in time be penetrated if fine quartz sand is used as an abrasive. Water added to the work in most forms of drilling speeds up the process but one must replenish it repeatedly in addition to keeping the hole clean if grit is to be kept from forming a thick paste and choking up the drill (Fig. 109).

Fig. 109. Using the pump drill

Another drill consists of a simple stick drill with a stone bit. This device is twirled between the hands. The simplest drill is merely a bit grasped in the fingers and twisted back and forth into the material being drilled.

Stone bits are usually necessary for getting the hole started. But after a shallow hole is formed in the stone, a bone or hardwood bit can be substituted, with sand serving as an abrasive. Bone and wood bits grip the grains of sand, causing them to cut rapidly into the stone. Water cannot be used with a wooden drill bit as it causes the wood to swell and bind.

## Stone Versus Steel

The utility of primitive stone tools compared to the utility of modern metal tools leaves little doubt as to which is superior. At the same time, however, stone cannot be regarded as totally inferior. For instance, flint arrowpoints are entirely equal to steel heads in their penetrating power; stone axeheads, though somewhat slower, will cut down a tree with as much sureness as the finest steel axe; a stone drill bit will make as neat a hole as a high-carbon steel bit; and a flint knife will skin a deer and cut it up just as well as a modern butcher knife.

Thus, it seems reasonable to a few artisans dedicated to primitive skills that mastery of the techniques of the Stone Age is imperative to true outdoor survival. A survivalist will not get very far if he uses methods that are not authentic, if, for instance, he believes that Indians made arrowheads with fire and a wet straw. But he can be master of almost any situation if he applies actual techniques.

## Working Bone

Cutting and carving bones into useful implements presents some special problems when one is working with stone tools only. But a few tips on handling bone-working implements will greatly reduce the time and sweat required to make a simple bone tool.

• For splitting bones, the tool of value is a graver, which one can make easily by flaking a small sharp nipple on the edge of a piece of hard stone, preferably agate or jasper. It is used to scratch a light groove down the length of a bone. The cut is then deepened with the application of rapid strokes made with the graver tip, the groove serving as a guide channel. This process is repeated on the opposite side of the bone.

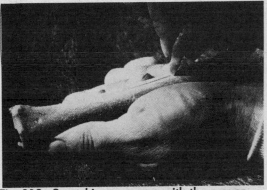

Fig. 110. Scratching a groove with the graver

Fig. 111. Tapping a grooved bone with a small rock

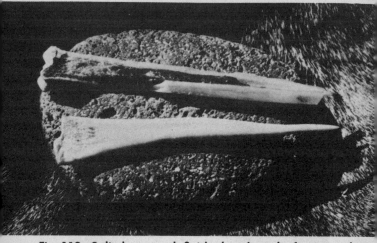

Fig. 112. Split bone and finished awl made from a split bone

Fig. 113. Sharpening a bone awl with a sanding stone

Next, the bone is placed on a stone and tapped with a small rock. The tapping is repeated all along the edges of the grooves until the bone splits (Figs. 110-12).

- For notching bones, a stone flake is needed. Sometimes one needs a bone tool with notches so that he can tie on strings or cut jagged edges, and these are easily carved with a stone flake.

- For sharpening and honing bones, a sanding stone is required (Fig. 113). The bone is rubbed back and forth on a rough stone surface and finished on a finer sanding stone. Small pieces of bone can be ground between two sanding surfaces. As the two stones are rubbed back and forth, the bone between them is ground rapidly.

- For drilling bones, the processes are exactly the same as those described for drilling stone (pp. 160-62.)

## Constructing Bows and Arrows

An archer under primitive conditions is somewhat different from the modern bowman with his laminated finery. His equipment even at best is vastly inferior, hence his success in hunting depends more on patience, practice, good luck, and a keen stalking ability that allows him close shots. But the value of the primitive bow and arrow must never be underestimated, as they are an important aid in filling the stewpot. The perfect shot quite often presents itself in the wilderness, and it is the wise hunter who has something to take the shot with (Fig. 114).

Fig. 114. Taking the shot

## Bows

The finest woods for making bows include mountain mahogany (*Cercocarpus*), ash (*Fraxinus*), service berry (*Amelanchier*), and chokecherry (*Prunus*). A sapling burned by a brush fire is excellent bow wood. Many trees uprooted by wind also have well-seasoned branches. But a dead tree with its roots still in the ground may be too brittle or too weathersplit for use, unless it has been killed by fire.

Since preseasoned wood is rare in the wilderness, green wood usually has to fill the need, and if carefully cured it is superior to other woods. A straight stave that is free from knots and small branches should be selected, and the stave should be carefully cut clear through, not broken off. It is the wise survivalist who selects two or three staves to work with—an extra bow stuck in the belt is good insurance.

The measurements of a bow will vary with the available supply, but too often staves are selected that are too large in diameter. The best diameter is from one to two inches at the handgrip. This must be determined *before* the bark is removed.

The length should be approximately 44 inches, but this will vary with each survivalist. A good method of determining length is for one to hold the stave on a horizontal plane extending from the left shoulder to the tip of the fingers of the extended right arm (Fig. 115).

Once the staves are selected and measured, the bark should be scraped off and left overnight in a cool but dry place. The staves must not be exposed to sunlight for the first six hours after the bark is removed.

The process of shaping a bow requires more than skill; it demands sensitivity and patience as well. Every stave, no matter how straight, has a natural bend to it which one can determine by placing the butt end on the ground and holding the stave vertical with his left hand in the middle where the handgrip will be. He then

Fig. 115. Determining the length of the bow

Fig. 116. Determining the natural bend of the bow

grasps the tip of the stave with his right hand and pulls it˙toward him lightly. The stave will turn in his left hand and settle into its natural bend. The side of the stave facing away from him then becomes the back of the bow (Fig. 116).

Only after the bend is determined should the actual shaping of the bow commence. Holding the stave with the butt, or larger, end pointing down, one can determine the exact location of the center of the handgrip and mark it with a scratch. Next he trims the upper half of the bow to the exact dimensions he desires, completing the top before starting the lower half. There is good reason for this which will become apparent if one does not comply with the directions.

Trimming the bow stave to its final dimensions should be done by sight alone. Each half is gracefully tapered from the center to the end in an even plane which results in a pointed tip. The circumference should be kept round from the handgrip to the tips. If the diameter of the bow is somewhat larger than expected, the belly of the bow can be flattened, but only to the degree that the bow becomes more flexible along its entire length.

One should never draw the bow during its construction to test it. Testing can be done by *slightly* bending the bow at intervals and judging its strength or stiffness by sight and weight. A good bow will look good and will be graceful and light.

The actual trimming and shaping process should *not* be done by whittling. Rather the excess wood should be scraped off in long even strokes from the handgrip to the tips (Fig. 117). A piece of flint, agate, jasper, or obsidian does the best job, but broken glass and steel knife blades are also effective. However, if one uses a knife blade he feels strongly tempted to speed up the process by whittling with it, and this ruins a bow stave. Most staves cut in the wilderness catch the blade and guide the cut in a spiral around them, thus causing the

Fig. 117. Scraping the bow staff

Fig. 118. Planing the bow with a flint chip

carver to remove too much wood in a small area and to make an uneven taper.

Holding a stone blade with sharp edges at a right angle to the stave, one can shave off thin strips of wood in much the same manner as when he uses a plane (Fig. 118). This tool is sometimes called a planar scraper or a flake blade (Fig. 119).

When the bow is finished it should be stored away for a day or two to cure. One can speed up the curing process, however, by holding the bow over hot coals or standing it by the fire.

When the bow is dry it should be greased with all of the animal fat it can absorb. The survivalist should then heat the bow and rub it until his arm aches. Fat can be obtained from any animal, even a mouse. If fat is not available, fish oil can be obtained from several chopped and boiled fish. The oil is skimmed off the water and rubbed on the bow. If oil is not available, the bow can be used as it is, and the survivalist can hope for a kill that will provide him with fat later on.

I was once severely criticized during a survival expedition by my companions and made to walk downwind from them for braving the stench of an old deer carcass to obtain some sinew and a chunk of rancid fat. However, they envied my efforts several days later when I completed a fine service berry wood bow and used the rancid fat and sinew to finish it off. We were miles away from the deer carcass by then and they gratefully shared my treasure for their own bows. After that we all smelled the same.

After his bow is cured and greased, the survivalist can give it a final shaping by recurving the tips. This in-

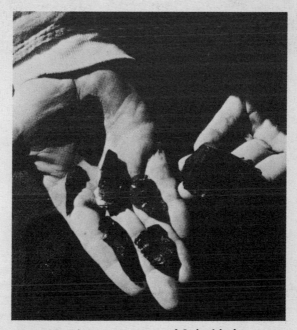

Fig. 119. Planar scrapers and flake blades

Fig. 120. Recurving the bow tips

Fig. 121. Roughening the bow tips

volves heating the tip of the bow over hot coals and then bending it over a smooth, round stone, holding it in position until it cools (Fig. 120).

The tips can be notched to receive the bowstring or left smooth. Smooth tips prevent splitting, but the tips should be scratched with a flint chip to roughen the surface, then smeared with hot, boiled pine pitch, and wrapped with sinew from the tip down, about three inches (Figs. 121-23). This provides a no-slip surface to tie the bowstring to and prevents the tips of the bow from splitting.

The bow is then strung when the string is tied permanently to one end, wrapped around the other end two or three times, and secured with two half hitches (Fig. 124).

The bow is now complete. It should be shot with the stave held on the same plane in which it originally grew in the bush—the butt end pointing down and the tip up. It should be kept unstrung when not in use and greased regularly (Fig. 125).

In a survival situation, a quickie bow, such as this, will do the job admirably for a patient and skilled hunter. The least amount of time in which it can be made is two days, if all the materials are available. Primitive man usually spent a great deal more time and consequently produced more lasting equipment, but it was not necessarily more effective.

The bow just described is capable of killing large game as well as rabbits, squirrels, and birds. But it is only as effective as its maker and user.

## Bowstrings

The strongest bowstrings are made from sinew (see Preparing Sinew, pp. 201-02), but nettle, milkweed, and some barks are usable substitutes, though inferior.

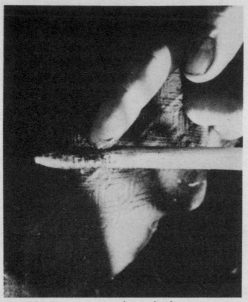

Fig. 122. Smearing pitch on the bow tip

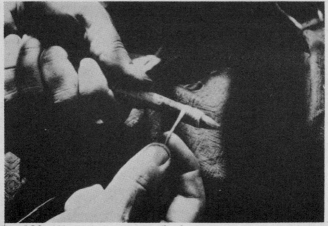

Fig. 123. Wrapping sinew on the bow tip

Fig. 124. Stringing the bow

Fig. 125. Finished bow

The string should be at least twelve inches longer than the bow.

Sinew strands are twisted together for bowstring in this manner: two strands of sinew are held in the left hand and pinched together between the thumb and second joint of the forefinger; then the strand that is farthest from the body is twisted clockwise with the right hand and then folded back over the second strand counterclockwise. This puts the second strand in the outside position to be twisted and brought back over the first one in the same manner. This process is continued until the required length is achieved. Splicing new length to the cord is done by carefully laying the new cord alongside the last inch of the old cord strand and twisting the two together. If the ends are carefully tapered for splicing with a sharp-edged tool, the diameter of the cord will not be increased (Figs. 126-30).

A sinew string is finished by stretching it between two points and rubbing saliva into it until all the rough spots are smoothed down. It must then dry in this position.

## Arrows

Several different kinds of serviceable arrow shafts can be constructed. Since feathers are at a premium in a wilderness situation, arrows are often made without them. And when feathers are available, glue for fletching them is sometimes not. Because of these limitations, one can see that methods of arrow production used under primitive conditions are vastly different from those used in ordinary circumstances. As a result the end products differ in many ways.

Arrows without fletchings are made from light woods and reeds. The common river reed (*Phragmites communis*) is best for such arrows. But willow (*Salix*) and

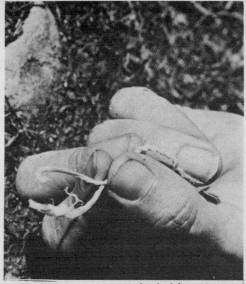

Fig. 126. Proper position for holding sinew

Fig. 127. Twisting counter-clockwise

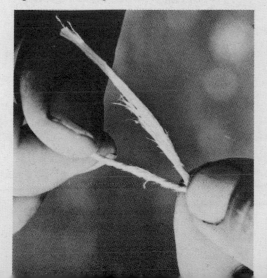

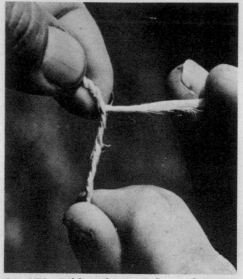

Fig. 128. Folding the twisted strand over the other strand

Fig. 129. Adding new strands to the cord

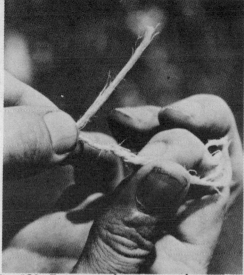

Fig. 130. Twisting in the new strands

Fig. 131. Preparing reeds for arrowshafts

a variety of light pithy woods can be used when reeds are not available (Fig. 131).

Reeds suitable for arrows are cut when dry. The length of each shaft should be about 24 inches, and the cuts should be made ½ inch above a joint on what will be the nock end and 3 or 4 inches below a joint on what will be the tip end (Figs. 132 and 134). This allows a strong place for the nock to be cut and leaves a hollow tube at the other end to receive a foreshaft. A reed shaft is straightened by rubbing grease (if available) on its joints and holding it over hot coals or on a hot rock until it is heated and then lightly bending it until it is straight, or as straight as one can make it (Fig. 133). It must be held in this position until it is cool. Reed stems are difficult to straighten between the joints, and one must be careful not to break them during the straightening process. Pitch is applied and sinew is wrapped around the tip end of the shaft to keep it from splitting. The nock is cut at the tip and wrapped with sinew for added strength (Fig. 134).

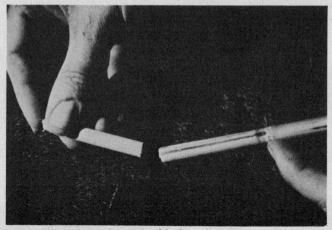

Fig. 132. Cutting the tip end below the joint

Fig. 133. Straightening the reed shaft

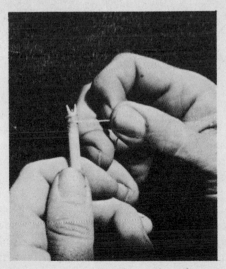

Fig. 134. Wrapping the nock end

Fig. 135. Completed arrow

Foreshafts are cut from any heavy hardwood tree or brush in 6- to 8-inch lengths. One end is sharpened to a point and hardened in a fire, and the other end is blunted and inserted into the hollow end of the reed stem. The arrow is then complete (Fig. 135).

These flimsy arrows are best used with a lightweight bow and prove effective for flock shooting and small game. A dozen or more of them can be made in one evening around the fire. They may last for only a few shots, but the simplicity and speed with which they are constructed makes them important and effective arrows. These same reed shafts can be made more accurate and deadly by the addition of stone points and fletchings (Fig. 136).

Woods best suited for sturdy hunting arrows are chokecherry (*Prunus*), service berry (*Amelanchier*), rose (*Rosa*), currant (*Ribes*), and willow (*Salix*). The shafts are selected from young shoots found in shaded areas where they must grow tall and straight to reach the sunlight. After they are cut, they must be dried in the sun for one day. The bark is then peeled and the still green shafts are cut into lengths several inches longer than the standard size for the finished arrows. Next, they are sorted according to size and weight, tied into bundles of five or six, and left to dry slowly in the shade for two days. One can speed up the drying process by placing the shafts in the sunlight or by holding

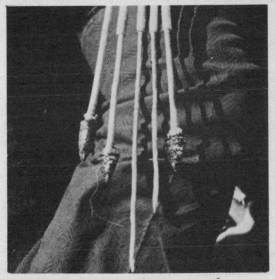

Fig. 136. Reed arrows with stone-tipped foreshafts

Fig. 137. Prying out crooks with an arrow wrench

them over hot coals, but the danger of splitting is increased when quick drying is used. However, effective arrow shafts can be turned out within a few hours after they are cut if they are dried with heat. It is very important that the shafts be completely dry before they are made into arrows. If one makes arrows in groups of five, completing each step with all five arrows before going on, much time is saved and the arrows are better matched for more accurate shooting.

Straightening wood shafts is simple and is done in the same manner as that described for straightening reed shafts. All one has to do is heat the crooked part and work it over his knee or with his fingers. An arrow wrench, which is a flat bone with a hole drilled in it, is also effective for prying out crooks (Fig. 137).

But one can get the job done much faster by gripping the shaft with his teeth just below the crook and then wrenching it straight with his hands (Fig. 138).

When the shafts are completely straight and dry, they are scraped down and smoothed with a chip of stone or broken glass (Fig. 139). Scraped lengthwise, the

Fig. 138. Straightening an arrow shaft

Fig. 139. Smoothing the arrow shaft

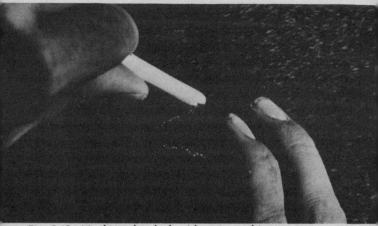

Fig. 140. Nocking the shaft with a stone chip

shafts become round and even. If a stone tip is to be used, the nock for the bowstring should be at the large end of the shaft. If the point is going to be simply sharpened and hardened in the fire, the nock should be made in the small end. Nocking the shaft for the bowstring is done by sawing the shaft with a sharp chip of stone (Fig. 140). The nock should be U-shaped and about ¼ inch deep.

Fletching an arrow by hand is not difficult if one uses glue. The feathers are bound in place until the glue dries and then the ends of the feathers are secured with sinew. Animal glue is made by boiling down hooves or fish skins. Some plants contain a sticky sap which is also effective. But pine pitch and plant sap are not good fletching materials.

Since animal glue is difficult to make, fletching without glue often becomes necessary in the wilderness. To accomplish this, one selects long feathers from the same bird wing or from the same side of the bird's tail. He then splits them down the center of the quill with a

fine chip of obsidian or other sharp stone. Next he sits
on the ground and holds one end of the feather on a
smooth rock with his big toe, and stretching the feather
taut with his left hand, he scrapes away the excess spine
with a sharp stone chip (Fig. 141). A little practice
will enable him to prepare feathers with professional
accuracy.

All of the feathers are then cut to the same length,
4 to 6 inches, and one inch of the web is stripped off
at the base. They are attached to the shaft in the following manner:

- First, one measures the point on the shaft that
  the web of the feather will reach when fully
  fletched.

Fig. 141. Scraping away the excess spine

- Then he measures up the shaft toward the *nock* about one inch—the distance from the tip of the stripped quill to the beginning of the web.
- He places one feather on the shaft upside down and inverts it so that the tip of its base is even with the one-inch mark on the shaft.
- He binds the stripped end of the feather to the shaft in this position, using only one or two wraps of sinew.
- He then places the other two feathers in the same position as the first feather and binds all of them down tightly with sinew, again using only one or two wrappings.
- He lifts each feather, bending the quill at the point where the web starts, and lays it flat against the shaft. The tips on the top end of the feathers he does not strip but lightly ruffles them back and dampens them with his fingers to hold them out of the way.
- He \wraps sinew over the ends of the feathers, just below the nock, leaving enough feather tip sticking out for him to grasp with his fingers.
- Grasping each tip with his fingers or with an improvised pair of pinchers, he pulls them tight, thus flattening the quill against the shaft and stiffening the vane.
- Finally, he wraps on additional sinew to secure the feathers tightly, allows the sinew to dry, and trims off the excess with a stone chip (Figs. 142-46).

A simpler method of fletching calls for a small amount of hot pine pitch to be smeared on the shaft where the ends of the feathers will be located and also just below the nock where the tip ends of the feathers will be bound. The pitch keeps the fletchings from pull-

Fig. 142. Measuring the web position

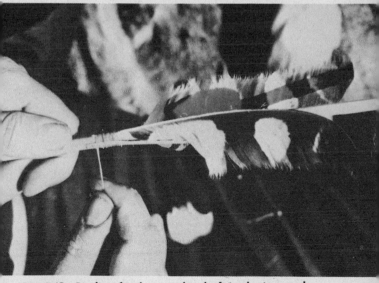

Fig. 143. Binding feathers to the shaft in the inverted position

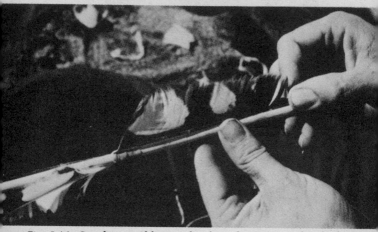

Fig. 144.  Bending and laying feathers flat against the shaft

Fig. 145.  Wrapping the ends of the feathers

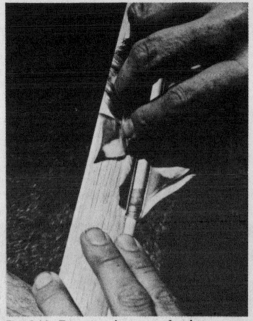

Fig. 146. Trimming the excess feathers

ing loose. The feathers are then pressed firmly into the warm pitch and wrapped with sinew. Next, the tip ends of the fletching are bound down and pulled to flatten the quill against the shaft (Figs. 147 and 148).

When one begins the process of attaching points, he discovers that filing a notch to receive a stone or bone point is hard work without a steel knife. It is much easier to break out a notch by using this old trick:

- A notch is cut on each side of the shaft at the point where the shaft length has been deter-

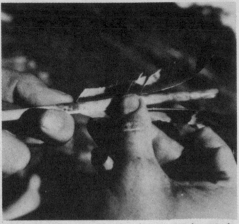

Fig. 147. Pressing the feathers into the pitch

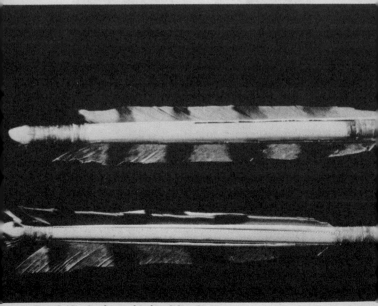

Fig. 148. Both methods of fletching

mined. This should present no problem because
the shaft was previously cut several inches longer
than was necessary.

- Another notch is cut on each side of the shaft
  between the first two notches ¼ inch above
  them.
- The excess shaft then breaks off when submitted
  to gentle pressure and bending, and a deep notch
  is left in the end which receives the head (Fig.
  149).

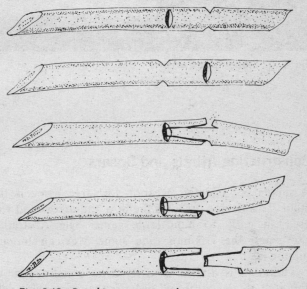

Fig. 149. Breaking out a notch

Before fitting the point to the shaft, one should
smooth and sand the notch to fit the contour of the
point. The point is then inserted in the notch, wrapped
with sinew, and, if possible, glued with pitch. When the
sinew is dry, the arrow is complete and ready for use
(Fig. 150).

Fig. 150. Stone-tipped arrows

## Constructing Atlatls and Spears

A simple but effective weapon for large game is the atlatl. This device predates the bow and arrow and was used anciently to hunt large game. The Australian aborigines, the Eskimos, and some Mexican Indians still use it.

The atlatl is a stick used to throw a light spear or dart with greater force and distance than is possible with just the arm. It acts as an extension to the arm, thus giving greater power to the thrower. The atlatl is about 2 feet long, 2 inches wide, and ½ inch thick. A prong is carved at one end to fit into the hollow butt of the spear, and 2 loops are tied at the other end through which the fingers of the thrower pass (Fig. 151).

The spear or dart is about 5 or 6 feet long with a

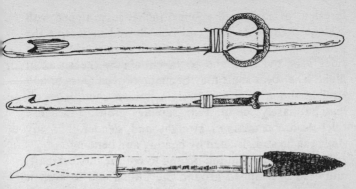

Fig. 151. Atlatl—throwing board and details of the spear foreshaft

Fig. 152. Finished spear

foreshaft of hardwood about 6 inches long, tipped with a stone point. The butt end is hollowed to receive the prong of the atlatl, and two feathers are tied to the sides near the butt end to help balance the spear in flight. The spear shaft may be made of reed grass or any straight shoot. A young straight juniper shoot is excellent but rarely found. Pine saplings growing in dense thickets are sometimes straight and slender, but any shaft can be straightened by heating and bending.

A hole is drilled in the tip end to receive the foreshaft, and cord is wrapped around the drilled end to keep it from splitting on impact. The feathering of the shaft need not be elaborate; two feathers tied securely with sinew at both ends and at the middle will do. The finished spear should be slender and not too heavy or cumbersome (Fig. 152).

Included here are a few suggestions which will aid the survivalist as he constructs the atlatl and spear:

- A natural bump or twig may be utilized for the prong on the atlatl.
- The wood is carved and shaped with stone tools in the same manner as that described for making arrows (pp. 176-85).
- Drilling a foreshaft socket is done best with a stone or bone drill set in the ground or held between the feet. The shaft is then twirled on it by being spun between the palms of the hands (Fig. 153).

Using the atlatl with skill demands much practice, and for this blunt spears without foreshafts should be used. They are also good for hunting small game. A snapping powerful throw is not necessary for using the spear. Rather it should be thrown overhanded with an even sweeping motion straight at the target, not lobbed

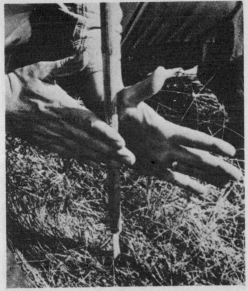

Fig. 153. Drilling a shaft by spinning it

Fig. 154. Correct position for throwing the spear or dart

Fig. 155. Throwing the spear or dart

over to it. When the butt end of the spear tends to dip down, thus spoiling its flight, it is a sign that the thrower is flipping it too hard or that the spear is too heavy (Figs. 154 and 155).

## Making Cordage

Strange as it may seem, a piece of string can become the most important item in a survival situation, for the construction of nearly everything requires this simple item. Equally surprising is the simplicity with which it can be manufactured in nature. Anything from sewing thread to rope can be made from a number of common wayside plants.

## Materials

Listed here are the common fibers which serve best for particular types of cordage. (The drawings in the Appendix will help you identify these plants.)

- Stinging Nettle, *Urtica*. The stalks of this plant contain a fiber that is very strong. When the stalks are dry, one pounds them to remove the woody parts and cleans the fiber by hand. It can be used to make such things as thread, fishline, string, yarn, snares, nets, ropes, cloth, bowstrings, sandals, blankets, and woven sacks.
- Milkweed, *Asclepias*. The stalks of this plant contain a silky fiber that can be used when the plant is green or dry. Best when harvested dry, it is processed in the same way as nettle and can serve for the same purposes.
- Dogbane, *Apocynum cannabinum*. This plant is perhaps the best fiber plant found in the West. The stalks contain a fine, soft, silky fiber that is easily worked. It is processed and used the same as are nettle and milkweed.
- Haw, Hawthorn, or Thornapple, *Crataegus*. The inner white bark of this plant makes good cordage. Though it cannot be used for as many different products as the fiber plants just listed, it can be stripped and twisted into string and rope and will serve in a pinch for fishline, snares, and sandals. The bark is strongest when wet and becomes a little stiff when dry. Other trees which have similar bark that is good for cordage are

willow, elm, spruce (roots), rose, and snow-berry.

- Sagebrush, *Artemisia tridentata*. This plant has a dry bark which can be stripped from the trunks and twisted into cordage. Though this bark is not strong, it has a wide variety of uses. It can be made into coarse woven bags and blankets and is the principal cordage for making sandals. The rope made from it is not very strong but will serve for tying things together and for hold-ing timbers in position for shelters. It may also be pounded and used for tinder. Other plants that have similar bark are juniper trees (*Juni-perus*) and cliffrose (*Cowania*). The barks of all these plants can be gathered in large quantities and used for bedding and thatching material.

## Twisting

After one has collected his materials, he is ready for the more involved part of making cordage. Listed here are the various steps involved in twisting fibers by hand—they are essentially the same steps as those discussed in the section on making bowstring (pp. 173-79).

- Two strips of fiber are selected and held in the left hand between the thumb and forefinger.
- The fiber farthest from the body is grasped in the fingers of the right hand and twisted clock-wise.
- The twisted strand is then laid counterclockwise over the other strand and becomes the one clos-est to the body.
- The second strand (now farthest from the body) is twisted and laid over the first strand in the

same manner. This is continued until the ends of the strands are reached.

- Other lengths of fiber are spliced on at this point. One does this by twisting the last two inches of the ends onto the new fibers and continuing the process of twisting and folding. It is best to alternate the lengths of the strands so that both splices do not appear at the same place in the finished string.

When short lengths of string are needed for tying something or sewing a few stitches, there is a quick way to produce them. The survivalist simply holds one end of a long strand in his left hand and rolls it in one direction on his thigh with his right hand. When it is rolled tight, he grasps one end in each hand and places the middle in his teeth. Then he puts the two ends together and holds them tightly. Next, he drops the end that is in his teeth and the string twines together automatically from the tension produced when it was twisted and rolled on the thigh. This results in a two-ply cord which is half the length of the original strand.

## Preparing Sinew

The long tendons from the legs of animals and the longer ones from their backs can be prepared and fashioned into cordage that is unequaled in strength. The best bowstrings are made from sinew (see Bowstrings, pp. 173-79). The simple strands also serve to haft arrowpoints and other tools to their wooden shafts. They are wrapped on while wet and do not need to be tied since the sinew is sticky enough to produce its own glue.

When the tendons are taken from the animal, they should be cleaned and placed in the sun until they are

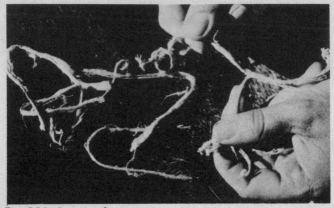

Fig. 156. Prepared sinew

completely hard and dry and then placed on a smooth rock and pounded with another rock until they are soft, fluffy, and white. The sinew will then strip apart into fine threads. It can be used dry for sewing thread, twisted into cords, or moistened for wrapping and hafting stone implements (Fig. 156).

## Weaving Clothes and Other Items

Like anything else that is worthwhile, weaving takes time. But a number of useful items can be made with the simple plain weave, an over-and-under technique. Cattail and bulrush stems produce good mats for floor coverings, beds, and shelter covers.

The twining method is used for making blankets, bags, sandals, fish traps, and some baskets. The foundation strands are called the warp and the interwoven strands are called the weft. There are two weft strands in twining, one going over the warp and the other under it, and they are crossed between each warp.

Most baskets used for water bottles and for carrying and harvesting seeds are made with the coiled technique. A basket is built up from the base with a growing spiral coil consisting of two small withes of willow and a bundle of fibrous material, usually grass or bark. Each coil is then stitched to the one below with a thin splint of willow or bark. The splint is passed through the coil with the aid of a bone awl (Fig. 157).

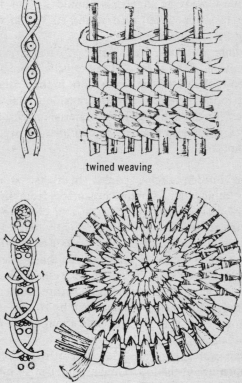

twined weaving

coiled weaving

**Fig. 157. Two major types of weaving**

There are some items and processes one should be aware of as he weaves which will make his work more efficient and save him time.

- Grasses and reeds selected for weaving should be dry and not green.
- The dried material should be soaked in water just before it is used and kept pliable during the weaving process.
- Willow weaving materials should be cut when green, stripped, left to dry, and soaked in water just before they are used.
- Splints are made from willows. The bark must be peeled from them and the outside layer of the wood taken off. The inside core is then used for the foundation rods and the outside or sapwood used for the splints. Other materials such as flat bark strips and rush strips can also be used for splints.

Large burden sacks, packs, blankets, storage-pit liners, clothing, and sandals are made from the inner soft bark of the cedar, sagebrush, and cliffrose plants. The strips of bark are fluffed and slightly twisted for the warp strands. Cords and flat strips are used for the weft. A loose twined weave is sufficient for the burden sacks and packs. Sandals are easily made from the bark in a few hours. Time does not usually permit refinement of the sandals, but serviceable ones can be twined in about three hours and will last through about three days of moderate use (Figs. 158-161).

Woven water jugs are merely coiled baskets with small openings at the top. They are lined with pitch that is smeared on the inside before the constricting top is made. The remainder is then lined in this way: a lump of pitch is placed inside the basket with a hot rock and the container is shaken until the pitch has melted and has spread over the surface. One prepares pine pitch by boiling lumps of it for about 15 minutes and then skimming off the surface with a flat stick. It must then be heated when used. Another method consists of burning the pitch on a sloping rock. The turpentine burns away, and the pure pitch runs down the rock to where it can be collected and molded into small balls.

Baskets can be made watertight without the pitch liner if they are constructed with a very tight coiled weave. The advantage of this is that one can boil water in them by merely placing hot stones in the baskets, a process called stone boiling. Food can also be prepared by the same stone boiling process, but instead of a basket a skin or a paunch is used.

Fig. 158. Blanket woven from bark

Fig. 159.  Size of woven blanket

Fig. 160.  Twined basket made from bulrush

Fig. 161. Sandals woven from bark

## Making Rawhide

Making good rawhide requires a little more care than just letting a green hide dry until it is stiff. Several steps must be taken to render it usable for moccasin soles, bags, pails, ropes, boxes, and other utilitarian items.

- The hide must be soaked in water a day or more if it has previously been dried out, but if it is green this step is not necessary.
- The hide is staked out with the flesh side up, and all of the fat and excess tissue is scraped off with a flesher, which is made from a long bone of a large animal. One side is honed down to a very sharp edge and small teeth are cut in it.

Then a strap is fastened to the top to serve as a wrist support. The implement is used in a hacking manner to peel and scrape the fat from the hide. Stone scrapers are held in the hand and applied in a drawing motion across the hide (Figs. 162-64).

- The hide is washed and cleaned and left staked out for a couple of days to dry in the sun. During the washing process the scrapers should be used to check that all fat is removed. Water is normally used for cleaning but better results can be achieved by using urine. This may be repulsive to most people, but it stands proven as a superior way of cleaning a hide. The urine should soak into the hide until the fat is completely dissolved by the strong acids. It is then scraped off, along with the dissolved fat. The urine cleaning is followed with a good washing of water.

- The hide, after it is dry and stiff and after the stakes are removed from it, is turned over and restaked. All of the hair is removed with a hair scraper. A sideways motion is used and every inch of the hide is covered. This back-breaking work is somewhat easier if the hide is soaked in a wood-ashes solution overnight. This loosens the hair and allows it to slip out rather than be shaved off by the hair scraper. Hair scrapers are simply small hoes made of wood, bone, or horn with a sharp stone blade attached to the hoe end. The blade must be sharpened often (Fig. 162).

- The final step in making rawhide is to place the dry hide on a soft pad of grass or old blankets and to pound it with a blunt stone hammer weighing about three or four pounds. The hide should be struck with short glancing blows, and every inch of it must be covered if the grain is to

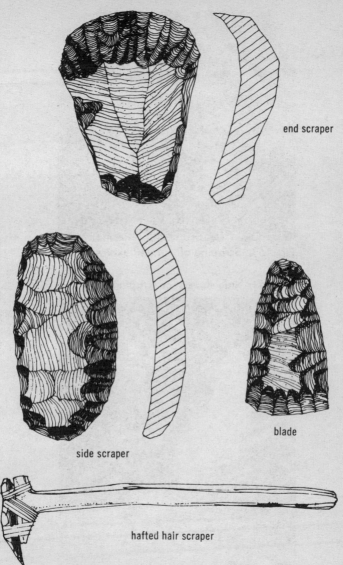

end scraper

side scraper

blade

hafted hair scraper

Fig. 162. Stone scrapers

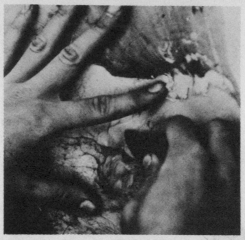

Fig. 163. Scraping off fat and excess tissue

Fig. 164. Hide staked for scraping

be broken and if the hide is to become white and soft. Rawhide prepared this way is just as tough as tanned shoe leather and almost as soft.

## Tanning Skins

Lightweight skins are tanned easily with or without the hair left on them. But hair that is hollow, such as that on deer, antelope, moose, and elk skins, must be removed. Tanning does not set the hair of these animals in the hide and it sheds continually. The hair is scraped off or slipped out in the same manner as that described

Fig. 165. Working the skin through a rope loop

under Making Rawhide (pp. 207-11). The hide is then put through the same soaking process as rawhide and the flesh is scraped off. Light skins such as deer and elk do not require the whitening, or pounding, process that is necessary for making rawhide.

The tanning agent used is usually the brain from the animal providing the hide, but any other brain will do. Generally the brain of the animal will be sufficient for tanning the entire hide. The time period involved from the moment of the kill until the hide is ready for tanning may be considerably longer than that for which most brains will remain fresh. But they can be preserved for use if they are lightly cooked and then sealed in a section of intestine. This is a very necessary precaution since there is nothing quite like ripe brains.

When the hide is ready for tanning, it should be staked out to dry. The warmed brains are finely mashed and rubbed on the skin with a smooth stone until they completely saturate it. Following this the skin is rolled up and placed in a warm place overnight. The next day the skin is staked out and scraped thoroughly until all excess brain tissue is removed. It is then worked back and forth through a rope loop, the friction of this action drying the hide and finishing the tanning process (Fig. 165).

If the hide is intended for clothing or moccasins, it should be smoked, for this allows the leather to dry soft again if it gets wet. The smoking process consists of draping the skin around a tripod under which is built a tiny smudge fire. This tepee arrangement allows the smoke to penetrate the skin quickly. The longer it is smoked the darker in color it becomes. A light buckskin brown indicates that it is smoked just the right amount.

# APPENDIX

The following drawings
identify numerous plants used
by the survivalist to fulfill
a variety of outdoor needs.

The pictures are
arranged alphabetically
by common name.
Appearing below
the common name(s)
are the scientific—
generic and species—
names (in italics). The
different uses of the plant—
as food, medicine, tinder, fiber—
are listed last.

The pictures of edible
plants are of specific
genera and species.
Therefore, in many
cases they are only

representative (being
among the most common
species growing in the
western United States)
of particular genera appearing
in the list of edible plants in
Chapter 5.

Some plants which are
edible are also poisonous
unless prepared
with caution; others
are easily confused with
poisonous plants.
Therefore, to aid
the reader and to caution
him, a † precedes
each of these.

**Amaranth**
*Amaranthus retroflexus*
Food

**Arrowhead**
*Sagittaria latifolia*
Food

**Arrowleaf Balsamroot**
*Balsamorrhiza sagittata*
Food

**Asparagus**
*Asparagus officinalis*
Food

**Beeplant**
*Cleome lutea*
Food

**Beeplant**
*Cleome serrulata*
Food

**†Biscuit-root**
*Cymopterus bulbosus*
Food, Medicine

**Blazing Star**
*Mentzelia laevicaulis*
Food

**Bluegrass**
*Poa longiligula*
Food

217

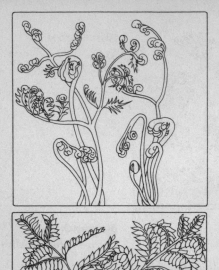

**†Bracken Fern**
*Pteridium aquilinum*
Food

**†Bracken Fern**
*Pteridium aquilinum*
Food

**Bristlegrass**
*Setaria viridis*
Food

**Bulrush**
*Scirpus*
Food, Fiber

**Bulrush**
*Scirpus acutus*
Food, Fiber

**Burdock**
*Arctium minus*
Food, Medicine

**Burdock**
*Arctium minus*
Food, Medicine

**Burreed**
*Sparganium
euricarpum*
Food

†**Camas**
*Camassia quamash*
Food

**†Camas**
*Camassia quamash*
Food

**†Camas—Death Camas**
*Zigadenus paniculatus*
Poisonous

**Cattail**
*Typha latifolia*
Food, Medicine, Tinder, Fiber, Tools

221

**†Chokecherry**
*Prunus virginiana*
Food, Medicine, Tools

**Cliffrose**
*Cowania mexicana*
Tinder, Fiber

**Cottonwood**
*Populus deltoides*
Food, Tinder

222

**Currant**
*Ribes*
Food, Tools

**Dogbane**
*Apocynum cannabinum*
Tinder, Fiber

†**Elderberry**
*Sambucus caerulea*
Food

223

†**Elderberry**
*Sambucus racemosa*
Food, Tinder

**Evening Primrose**
*Oenothera hookeri*
Food

**Goldenrod**
*Solidago*
Food

224

**Ground Cherry**
*Physalis fendleria*
Food

**Groundsel**
*Senecio*
Food

**Hairgrass**
*Deschampsia
elongata*
Food

225

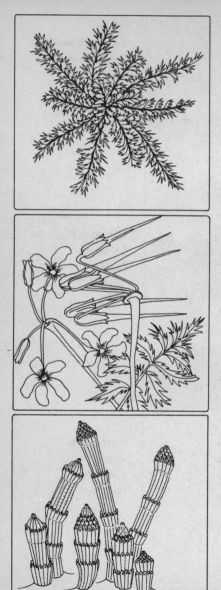

**Heron's Bill**
*Erodium cicutarium*
Food

**Heron's Bill**
*Erodium cicutarium*
Food

**Horsetail**
*Equisetum hyemale*
Food

**Indian Potato**
*Orogenia linariifolia*
Food

**Indian Potato**
*Orogenia linariifolia*
Food

**Indian Ricegrass**
*Oryzopsis
hymenoides*
Food

227

**Jerusalem
Artichoke**
*Helianthus tuberosus*
Food

**Jerusalem
Artichoke**
*Helianthus tuberosus*
Food

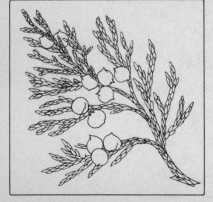

**Juniper**
*Juniperus
osteosperma*
Food

**Juniper**
*Juniperus osteosperma*
Food, Tinder, Fiber

**Lamb's Quarter**
*Chenopodium album*
Food

**Mallow**
*Malva neglecta*
Food

229

**Maple**
*Acer negundo*
Food

†**Milkweed**
*Asclepias speciosa*
Food, Fiber

**Miner's Lettuce**
*Montia perfoliata*
Food

230

**Mint**
*Mentha*
Food

**Mint**
*Mentha*
Food

**Mint**
*Nepeta cataria*
Food

231

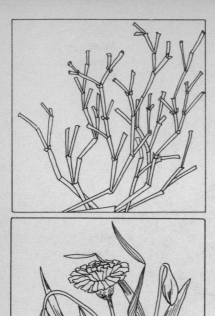

**Mormon Tea**
*Ephedra*
Food

**Mountain Dandelion**
*Agoseris aurantiaca*
Food

**Mule's Ears**
*Wyethia amplexicaulis*
Food

232

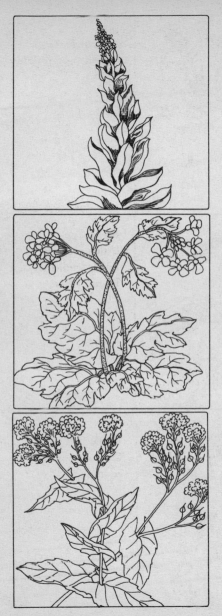

**Mullein**
*Verbascum thapsus*
Medicine, Tinder

**Mustard**
*Brassica nigra*
Food

**Mustard**
*Cardaria draba*
Food

**Mustard**
*Lepidium perfoliatum*
Food

**Nettle**
*Urtica gracilis*
Food, Medicine,
Tinder, Fiber

†**Oak**
*Quercus gambelii*
Food

†**Onion**
*Allium acuminatum*
Food, Medicine

†**Onion**
*Allium textile*
Food, Medicine

**Oregon Grape**
*Mahonia aquifolium*
**Food**

**Oregon Grape**
*Mahonia fremontii*
Food

**Piñon Pine**
*Pinus edulis*
Food

**Plantain**
*Plantago lanceolata*
Food, Medicine

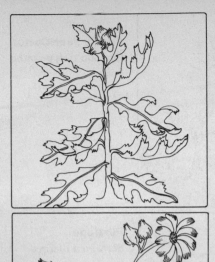

**Prickly Lettuce**
*Lactuca scariola*
Food

**Prickly Lettuce**
*Lactuca scariola*
Food

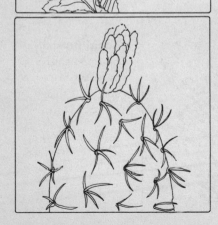

**Prickly Pear Cactus**
*Opuntia
phaeacantha*
Food

237

**Prickly Pear Cactus**
*Opuntia polyacantha*
Food

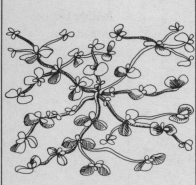

**Purslane**
*Portulaca oleracea*
Food

**†Rabbitbrush**
*Chrysothamnus
nauseosus*
Food

238

**Raspberry**
*Rubus idaeus*
Food

**Red Clover**
*Trifolium pratense*
Food

**Reed**
*Phragmites communis*
Food, Tinder,
Fiber, Tools

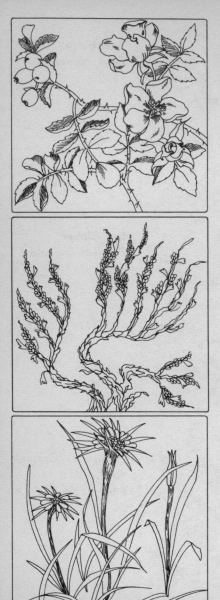

**Rose**
*Rosa*
Food, Medicine, Tools

**Sagebrush**
*Artemisia tridentata*
Tinder, Fiber

**Salsify**
*Tragopogon dubius*
Food

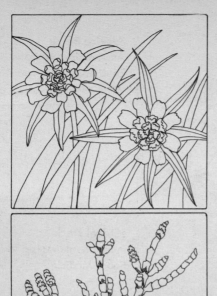

**Salsify**
*Tragopogon dubius*
(yellow)
*Tragopogon
porrifolius* (purple)
Food

**Samphire**
*Salicornia pacifica*
Food

**Sego Lily**
*Calochortus nuttallii*
Food

**Service Berry**
*Amelanchier alnifolia*
Food, Medicine, Tools

†**Sorrel Dock**
*Rumex hymenosepalus*
Food, Medicine

†**Sour Dock**
*Rumex crispus*
Food, Medicine

242

**Spring Beauty**
*Claytonia lanceolata*
Food

**Strawberry**
*Fragaria vesca*
Food

**Sumac**
*Rhus trilobata*
Food

243

**Sunflower**
*Helianthus annuus*
Food, Tinder

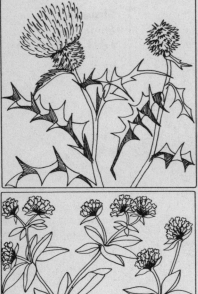

**Thistle**
*Cirsium undulatum*
Food, Tinder

**Umbrella Plant**
*Eriogonum alpinum*
Food

**Violet**
*Erythronium
grandiflorum*
Food

**Watercress**
*Rorippa
nasturium-aquaticum*
Food

**Waterleaf**
*Hydrophyllum
capitatum*
Food

**†Wild Hyacinth**
*Brodiaea douglasii*
Food

**Yarrow**
*Achillea millefolium*
Medicine

**Yellow Fritillary**
*Fritillaria pudica*
Food

# INDEX